THE SACRED LITERATURE SERIES

SOLOMON'S RING

*The Sacred Literature Series of
the International Sacred Literature Trust*

TADHKIRA GHAUTHYA

Solomon's Ring

The Life and Teachings of a Sufi Master

Gul Hasan

Selected, translated and introduced
by Hasan Askari

ALTAMIRA
PRESS
A Division of Sage Publications, Inc.
Walnut Creek • London • New Delhi

Funded by
THE
ARTS
COUNCIL
OF ENGLAND

For more information about the
International Sacred Literature Trust,
please write to the ISLT at:
22 Northumberland Avenue, London WC2N 5AP,
United Kingdom

For information address:
AltaMira Press
A Division of Sage Publications, Inc.
1630 North Main Street, Suite 367
Walnut Creek, CA 94596, USA
explore @ altamira.sagepub.com

SAGE Publications Ltd
6 Bonhill Street
London EC2A 4PU
United Kingdom

SAGE Publications India Pvt. Ltd.
M-32 Market
Greater Kailash 1
New Delhi 110 048, India

Photoset in Sabon by Northern Phototypesetting Company Limited, Bolton, UK

PRINTED IN THE UNITED STATES OF AMERICA

98 99 00 01 02 03 04 05 06 07   7 6 5 4 3 2 1

Library of Congress Cataloging-in-Publication

Qādirī, Sayyid Shāh Gul Hasan Qalandarī
    [Tazkirah-yi Ghausiyyah. Selections. English]
    Solomon's ring = Tadhkira Ghauthya : the life and teachings of a Sufi
master / Gul Hasan ; selected, translated, and introduced by Hasan Askari.
    p. cm. —(Sacred literature series)
    ISBN 0-7619-8983-8 (cloth : alk. paper). —ISBN 0-7619-8984-6 (pbk.
: alk. paper)
    1. Qalandar Pānīpatī, Ghaus 'Alī Shāh, 1804-1880. 2. Sufism—India.
I. Title. II. Series.
BP80. Q35Q23213   1998
297.4'092—dc21
[B]   98-10267
                                                                 CIP

INTERNATIONAL
SACRED
LITERATURE
TRUST

The International Sacred Literature Trust was established to promote understanding and open discussion between and within faiths and to give voice in today's world to the wisdom that speaks across time and traditions.

What resources do the sacred traditions of the world possess to respond to the great global threats of poverty, war, ecological disaster and spiritual despair?

Our starting-point is the sacred texts with their vision of a higher truth and their deep insights into the nature of humanity and the universe we inhabit. The translation programme is planned so that each faith community articulates its own teachings with the intention of enhancing its self-understanding as well as the understanding of those of other faiths and those of no faith.

The Trust particularly encourages faiths to make available texts which are needed in translation for their own communities and also texts which are little known outside the tradition but which have the power to inspire, console, enlighten and transform. These sources from the past become resources for the present and future when we make inspired use of them to guide us in shaping the contemporary world.

Our religious traditions are diverse but, as with the natural environment, we are discovering the global interdependence of human hearts and minds. The Trust invites all to participate in the modern experience of interfaith encounter and exchange which marks a new phase in the human quest to discover our full humanity.

A story is a tree that grows in the soil of the heart.

In memory of my father
Ali Naqi

ABOUT THE TRANSLATOR

Professor Hasan Askari is a Sufi sociologist, philosopher, and poet from Hyderabad, India. His native language is Urdu. He has taught at many universities: Osmania (India), Beirut, Aligarh, Amsterdam, Birmingham—and has been a Visting Professor at Antwerp and Denver. He has also given special lectures at the universities of Tehran, Frankfurt, Heidelburg, Mainz, Gottingen, Rome, Utrecht, Leiden, Aberdeen, Oxford, Cambridge, Harvard, Uppsula, and Stockholm.

He is well known as one of the pioneers and truly original thinkers of inter-religious dialogue and has been a notable player at international conferences and seminars since the early 70s. He is named in Bishop Kenneth Cragg's *Pen and the Faith* (Allen & Utwin 1984) as one of the top eight Muslim thinkers of the century.

His many books include *Speeches of Ali ibn Abi Talib; Spiritual Quest: an Interreligious Dimension, Alone to Alone: From Awareness to Vision, Seers and Sages (600 BC - 1950 AD), The Experience of Religious Diversity, The Essence of Plotinus; Soul-Beings: Reflections and Meditations*, and *First Soul, then God.*

Contents

Acknowledgments

I recall with gratitude Jane Amphlett, who regularly encouraged me to continue the present work. Most of the stories were initially edited by her. I am also indebted to Ayesha Johnson for her useful suggestions and help with editing. I am grateful to Musa Askari for his continuous assistance in preparing the manuscript and to Jenny Litaba for her meticulous work proofing it.

Hasan Askari

We thank our readers, Professor B. Sheik Ali, former Vice-Chancellor of Mangalore and Goa Universities; Professor Nisar Ahmed Faruqi, Head of the Department of Arabic, University of Delhi; Madan Gupta, writer and translator in New Delhi; and Dr Mukhtar Uddin Ahmed of Yorkshire, England. We gratefully acknowledge M. Ramachandran for his work assisting us to contact the readers in India. Our thanks also to Alison Forbes and Wendy Clifford, both of whom worked on the administration of the book, and, as always, to Quentin Smith and Doreen Mantle for their continued support.

International Sacred Literature Trust

Translator's Introduction

*It is evident truth, that the Supreme is everywhere and yet
nowhere. Keeping this constantly in mind let us see
how it bears on our present inquiry.*

Plotinus, *Enneads* 6.8.16

He is the first and the last, the hidden and the manifest.

Qur'an 57.3

Some books appear like comets in the firmament of one's mind
as omens of events and developments that will have shattering
as well as transforming effect. Such was the feeling of expansion in
my soul when I came across the strange book which is now presented here. It was in the late sixties while I was still in India that
I heard of *Tadhkira Ghauthya*, the first book of its kind in Urdu. It
recounted the life and teachings of a Sufi Master, Ghauth Ali Shah
Qalander (1804–1880), composed by one of his direct disciples, Gul
Hasan.

The late sixties were a time in my life when I was going through
far-reaching inner changes. They were being reflected in people
whom I met, in books I read, and in lectures I gave. I was search-
ing for a theology of religious diversity, for a philosophy that could
explain the spiritual necessity of more than one religious form.
Although certain ideas in contemporary Western philosophy gave
me a clarity and strength of understanding, they seemed to skirt
around the challenge of personal spirituality in a multifaith society.
I was looking for a language which could make dialogue possible
and mutually enriching between people of different religious traditions. I was already free from sectarian and religious dogmatism;
had turned my back upon all polemical discourse. Real speech was
for me a linking of soul with soul. Before I could experience the
birth of a new speech within myself, I needed a conceptual founda-

tion, the relevant intellectual clarity.

Increasingly dissatisfied with the sociology of religion, I was drawn into the Jungian perspective on symbols and their roots in the collective unconscious. But, however enriching my initial contact with Jungian psychology, it did not have an uplifting effect upon my soul; I sensed Jung's deep ambiguities of both a philosophical and a spiritual nature. I was distressed at his resistance to metaphysics, and appalled at the way he imposed his own ideas in his commentaries on the *Tibetan Book of the Dead* and also *The Secret of the Golden Flower*. I felt a greater clarity in Cassirer's philosophy of symbolic forms whereby all forms, from myth to philosophy and science and from religion to art and poetry, were functions of the spirit of humanity, each valid and adequate as a form of the soul's creative and self-conscious energy.

But it was Wilfred Cantwell Smith, whom I first met in 1965 and then again in 1968 at a seminar in Bangalore, who gave me the insight and direction I was seeking. When I attended that seminar in Bangalore I had no idea that it would open a new path for me and bring me into the very heart of the interfaith dialogue across continents. Smith's distinction between faith and belief provided me with a foundation to relate positively to "the other". While belief is a part of the cumulative tradition, faith is the personal immediate possession of each individual by which one relates to one's life, to all those whom one encounters, faith being a vast world in which all can participate. Faith is thus an inner ability to relate and communicate without fear. I now had a spiritual basis to respect and listen to others.

This realization was an inner voice, clear and yet solitary. Neither among the social scientists at the university nor with the politicians and writers I met in the city was there any concern for the theological and mystical foundations for a multi-religious society. It was assumed that, with secular democracy and economic development, India's religious and cultural problems would be solved. But as years went by, Hindu–Muslim riots increased. Both Hindu and

Muslim fundamentalism became more organized and militant. Their intermittent appeals to people's humanity and moral values during times of communal tension were, at best, cries of despair; otherwise mere platitudes. It was amidst this spiritual vacuum and intellectual barrenness that I was being constantly drawn to reflect upon the inter-religious dimension, its theological and mystical, philosophical and political importance.

As if by divine providence I was invited to a conference on inter-faith issues held in Lebanon in March 1970 where I met people from Europe and America who were seriously thinking about inter-religious questions. To encounter so many kindred spirits was an experience that I will never forget, and it was then that I became part of the international movement of dialogue between living faiths. When I returned to India I was depressed, feeling there was nothing there for me to rely upon and draw inspiration from. I required a model from within my own country. True, there were examples in medieval India of eclectic princes, great Sufi masters and Bhakti poets who represented the same voice that was within my heart. But I was looking for a life lived fully in the depths of both Hindu and Muslim spirituality.

It was then in the summer of that same year that *Tadhkira Ghauthya* came into my hands. It was an old edition dated 1898, its binding and paper worn out. To hold it was like holding an old silver coin bearing the insignia of a long-forgotten kingdom, a currency which was no longer in circulation. There was an air of friendship and trustworthiness about the book. While turning its pages I used to experience a fragrance like that of dried rose petals, as if before the eye of my soul the doors of a rose garden were opening.

Behind the veil of several discourses and stories, there, spread before me, was a life full of the authenticity of encounter with various expressions of spiritual life from Muslim theologians to Sufi masters, from Hindu pandits to *sanyasis* (ascetics), from sober scholars to "madmen" who conceal beneath their madness great treasures of gnosis. Some stories were hilarious and yet there seemed to be buried beneath their surface profound hints for unravelling some mystery. The cultural canvas of the stories covered a baffling vastness from Asia Minor to Persia to the Indus Valley and the Gangetic plain. The characters represented diverse cultures and religions. The Islamic and Vedantic threads were so interwoven as to constitute one fabric. There it was, within that book: a life I was seeking, right from within the Indian context, to hold a mirror to my own inner vision of interfaith spirituality and ultimately of a dimension that transcends religion.

It tells of the life and teachings of a *qalander*, a spiritual nomad, who comes home through homelessness. Though initiated into all major Sufi orders, and living by the inner and the outer discipline of Islam, he had received many lessons from the Hindu *rishis* (sages) and had reached a point within himself which transcended both. His biographer, Gul Hasan, speaks in the language of the heart. The way the book opens and closes bears testimony to a soul that had tasted the nectar of self-realization in the company of his master. Ghauth Ali Shah was for him as Socrates was for Plato, as Ammonius Saccas was for Plotinus. The relationship of master to disciple in the Orient is that of a lamp from which other lamps are lit; it is of a fragrance which fills those who come into its vicinity with freshness of being and remembrance of the rose of primeval unity. It is freedom from bondage, even from that of obedience to the authority of the master. Hence, in the fellowship of Ghauth Ali Shah, we find friendship more than discipleship in its traditional sense. There is no secret society, no closed occult rite, no psychological control of the initiates – stories are the teachers, and discourses are the disciples. In each seeker, including Ghauth Ali Shah, there is this link of the contemplative through storytelling with that of the reflective mode through discourses. This is the inner discipleship. Reason, as a disciple of contemplative intellect, resides in the soul of each human. On the outer level there is hospitality and openness of heart.

Ghauth Ali Shah's life covers almost the entire span of the nineteenth century from 1804 to 1880, a time of massive upheavals and revolutions. The British power had already spread from Bengal to the whole of north India. The last symbol of the Mughal empire, Emperor Bahadur Shah Zafar, was confined to his fort in Delhi, and that last symbol also was wiped out in 1857. India had now become part of the British Empire. The consequences for the Muslims of India were tremendous. Once a ruling class, they were now a displaced, disheartened and defeated minority locked within the massive, now increasingly self-conscious Hindu majority. There were attempts made by certain Muslim intellectuals during that period, particularly those who were led by Syed Ahmad Khan, to provide self-confidence to the Muslims and to help them adjust to the new political situation. There was also a miraculously supreme creative outburst of Urdu poetry, especially in Ghalib (one of the great Urdu poets of the nineteenth century), which both reflected the melancholy of the Muslim soul and also transcended it.

The elegance of the Muslim society reflected in Lucknow and Delhi was the last glitter of a decadent culture. The socio-economic world of the Muslims presented the image of a shipwreck. Muslim landlords and princes floated on larger pieces of the wreckage, but the vast majority of the Muslims were thrown into a dangerous sea of economic and social uncertainty. Yet, amidst all that upheaval, we notice the life of the common people, both Hindu and Muslim, continuing with a strange informality and serenity. It to this current of life that Ghauth Ali Shah was deeply attuned and it was in that vast ocean of the Indian psyche that he swam like a dolphin. His stay at Panipat, a few miles outside Delhi, is reminiscent of the story of Plotinus outside Rome, one witnessing the edifice of the Mughal Empire being razed to the ground, and another watching the tottering Roman Empire. Unlike Plotinus, Ghauth Ali Shah shows an acute sense of history as a sign of God's power over the nations of the world. He was aware that the hundreds of people who approached him for their needs and problems were all victims of an historical catastrophe. He also knew that most of their requirements were psychological; they required consolidation and he gave it to them. He saw the divide between the Hindu and Muslim communities increasing, polemicism rising, and it broke his heart.

Surrounded by the challenges of his times, he remained calm, his attention focused on the transcendence of All-Being. He not only travelled from place to place but was a nomad through history, understanding that all times were one time, one moment, in the powerful hands of God. He knew that beyond fear and hope, distraction and concentration, beyond all distress or fulfilment, all have one Source of Being, one love by which their hearts are broken, by which their hearts are joined.

The significance of the book for my own inner journey can be summed up by citing an episode from the first half of the nineteenth century from the city of Lucknow. It sums up the entire hermeneutic challenge of religious symbolism, which is the main thrust of Ghauth Ali Shah's life and message. The episode is as follows.

Every Thursday evening a fellowship of spiritual seekers would meet. Abdur Rahim Khan-e-Khanan, a renowned mystic and poet, was a member of that fellowship. One Thursday evening as they assembled, one of them said, "Friends, I have a dream to share." Others waited with their usual calm and grace. "I saw a vast open space," he began, "and there was a great fire raging. I saw the figure of Krishna right in the middle of that fire, and the figure of Ram outside the circle of fire as if he was about to enter."

One of them immediately responded, "Is it not obvious what the dream means? The fire you saw was the fire of hell; Krishna has already been thrown into it and Ram was soon to join him."

At this daring interpretation there was an air of unrest in the fellowship. Abdur Rahim Khan-e-Khanan, the mystic and poet, was sitting with his head bowed, his hands joined resting in his lap. After a long pause he lifted his head and looked towards the person who had interpreted the dream, and with a gentleness and clarity that shone like a sword of light, he said, "Friend, if you allow me, I should say that you have committed two very grave mistakes: first, you have abused the figures which our Hindu brethren hold in great respect and devotion, and this is morally wrong from the Islamic point of view, and also generally we should not speak ill of someone else's beloved. The second mistake you have committed is spiritual; you have shown a strange haste in interpreting a dream which should be regarded as a sign from the realm of the unseen."

The fellowship, thus alerted by these words of wisdom, felt refreshed as if a heavy burden had been lifted from their souls. They all looked at Abdur Rahim Khan-e-Khanan sitting once more with bowed head, hands together in his lap. He lifted his head again and said, "Friends, there is another way to look at the dream. Let us regard the fire you saw in your dream as the fire of love; then we understand that Krishna, being the archetype of perfection in love, should be in the centre of that fire, and Ram, being yet a novice and a seeker, was seen still standing outside the fire."

When two spiritual cultures meet, a hermeneutic challenge is born. The fate of each one of those cultures depends upon how one interprets the other's symbolic language. As in an individual's dream, so in a collective dream of our life in this world, there are signs to be interpreted and integrated into our consciousness. It appears that from the nineteenth century onwards the hermeneutic challenge before the Hindus and Muslims of India consisted of two options – one literal, closed and mutually destructive, and the other, symbolic, open-ended and mutually constructive. Through India's long history, the latter option has enjoyed wide currency, allowing the traditions of the country to flourish. But, since the nineteenth century, we have been watching the option of division and conflict take over. The hermeneutics of the heart that transcends the literal mode of understanding was, and remains, within our reach. Ghauth Ali Shah through his life, discourses and stories represents that creative option.

Over the following years I reflected upon the book that portrays his life and message. Each time new meanings would leap up from the text, new vistas unfold before the eye of the heart. After a couple of years something strange happened which I would like to place on record. The book was usually kept in a bookshelf built into the wall of my small study. For a few weeks I had not looked at the book nor did I open that particular cupboard. One afternoon as I slept I had a dream. I was standing in a well-lit hall and I heard someone telling me that the man sitting at the far end of the hall was Ghauth Ali Shah. Then I found my father, who had passed away some fifteen years previously, standing beside me. We both started walking towards Ghauth Ali Shah. We greeted him and he greeted us. I noticed behind him a light blue curtain and from behind the curtain I heard strange music whose melody was unlike anything I had heard before.

When I woke up I was puzzled. I tried to understand the dream, to know what it represented, but it remained a mystery. After a few minutes, I thought of consulting the book to see if any of its stories could help me unravel the dream. When I reached for the bookshelf and opened it, I saw the entire book covered with termites. They had already eaten the binding and the margins of the pages and were about to eat the words. I extracted the book from the tight grip of the termites, cleared it and then realized that the dream was given to draw attention to the book, and to save it.

The experience of being directed through a dream to save the book strengthened my faith in the connection of souls on either side of the frontier of death. In reality, there is no death as far as soul is concerned, and hence, those who are awake and advanced in knowledge, irrespective of whether they are still alive or have passed away from this world, constitute one living unity of knowledge. There is no question of a teacher being dead – all teachers are alive.

A book written by a sage is like the residence in which he still lives. We all experience such living presence, whether we enter Rumi's *Mathnawi* or *The Enneads* of Plotinus. Such was and has been my experience with the memoirs of Ghauth Ali Shah.

Though the book as presented here will speak for itself, let us however now focus on certain ideas which are crucial to its basic message.

Religion

The very first fact about Ghauth Ali Shah's life, as given by Gul Hasan, is extraordinary, particularly in view of contemporary Muslim fundamentalism. We are told that Ghauth Ali Shah was fed during his infancy by a Hindu wet nurse, recommended by his grandfather. She was a pious God-fearing woman, the wife of a pandit, probably a *brahmin*. At the beginning of the nineteenth century there were many Muslims who had a very different approach to religious purity. For Ghauth Ali Shah's grandfather, purity was inner purity anchored in personal piety. It was within this spiritual ethos that Ghauth Ali Shah grew up, and therefore it was with great ease that he could sit at the feet of both the Hindu rishis and the Muslim masters in his later life.

But the challenge now, as then, pertains to the relationship between the form of a given religion and the formless Reality of which that religious form is a symbol. It was one of the most powerful achievements of both the Bhakti (devotional Hindu) and the Sufi (mystical Islamic) orders of medieval India that they looked at the religious form as a garment which this soul had donned for her journey through this world in one culture or another. As in the event of death, we leave our body here, so also we leave our religious garment. What ultimately remains with the soul is her grade of purity and station of knowledge. Ghauth Ali Shah, through his long acquaintance with both the Vedantic and the Islamic modes of meditation, agreed with those who held that one could rise above one's physical and religious form in deep contemplative moments. Those who have not yet fully realized the transcendental Unity of God return to the memory of their religious tradition as they come out of their meditations. As one sacrifices one's wealth to save one's life, or sacrifices one's life to save the lives of those whom one loves, so one sacrifices one's religion in order to draw nearer to God. Between the highest state of attaining to the Formless Reality and the lowest state of remaining identified with one or another religious form, there is a vast world of imagination.

Religious Imagination

One of the unique features of Ghauth Ali Shah's perspective on religious matters is his view of imagination as a principle and a power. It is also the ultimate barrier in the soul's ascent to its Ultimate Source. Imagination rests on the imaging principle by which an idea assumes a form whether in thought or in the material world. As a power, it is the soul's act and also one of the reasons for her imprisonment.

We are told through several discourses that each religious form, besides giving signs of the ultimate Reality, rests on a collective imagination, and most people project images derived from their environment and culture to describe the Reality beyond the sensible world. The way they understand God and picture the images of life hereafter may all be regarded as a work of the religious imagination linked with the collective culture and also with the particular emotional needs of the individual.

Then Ghauth Ali Shah refers to the role of the mystical discipline in liberating the novice from the collective religious imagination. If the mystical orders, by doctrine or by practice, enforce the collective culture of the novice then there is something fundamentally wrong with their understanding of the ultimate goal of the path of mystical life. Ghauth Ali Shah notices during his encounters with several powerful men how some of their practices were restricted to strengthening one's attachment to one's own religious forms, figures and symbols.

There is, however, an important function of the imaging principle in one particular mystical practice, namely meditation on the image of one's own spiritual guide. This is recommended to enable the novice to transcend his or her ego and persona and connect with the guide so that an inner path is opened between them for communicating guidance and support. But there is an underlying mystery in this particular mystical practice. The image of the teacher within the mind of the novice is also a point of contact between their souls at the frontier of the imagination. The novice is thus brought to the ultimate barrier with the help of the guide, at which point the guide self-annihilates and thus both step into the realm which is beyond all imaging.

Ghauth Ali Shah points out that each soul, here in body, is under some dominant mode of her imagination. It is this dominant mode which describes her life here and also the kind of world that the soul will enter after her body's death. Hence there is neither hell nor heaven but only what one brings through one's dominant mode of imagination. Here Ghauth Ali Shah cites the Prophet's tradition that God is as His servant imagines Him to be (see p. 36).

There is, however, another mystery which underlies this relationship between imagination and life, both here and hereafter. One may perhaps think that nothing is real beyond this world, such things as heaven and hell are a fantasy and an illusion, as if the scriptures are all false. Or one may take the view that everything is symbolic without any literal connotations. It is this challenge which has troubled religious thought throughout the centuries, resulting in the diametrically opposed schools of literalism and symbolism, not to speak of those who reject outright every religious belief.

Ghauth Ali Shah unties this knot in one of his unique ways. The first postulate is that all is real, for all issues from the Reality of the Supreme Source. Whatever is manifested both in the sensible world and in the world of imagination is under one attribute or another of the same Reality whether you call it God or refer to it by any other name. Every form of life, every idea and every image is an attribute of the same Eternal Essence. So also the dominant mode of imagination under which one lives, under which one entertains hopes and fears. As humanity is given free will under the divine attribute of freedom, we are free to choose our own dominant mode of imagination, our own destiny. At this stage we notice that two mystical paths appear before the seeker: the path of divine attributes and the path above it, that of Divine Essence. Attributes manifest the essence and essence both holds and envelopes the attributes. Where one begins, where one ends, there is neither any knowledge nor any utterance about its mystery. Hence, the Qur'an says, *He is the first and the last, the hidden and the manifest* [Q. 57.3]. Everything at once!

Throughout his life, Ghauth Ali Shah's basic focus was on how one transcends the realm of the attributes to enter and merge with the realm of the Essence. For him, all philosophy, all religion and all mysticism are intended for that final breakthrough. It is her own dominion in which the divine attributes are manifested that the soul, yearning to unite with the Supreme Source, strives to leave behind.

Whether one is immersed in the realm of the divine attributes or moves beyond them towards the realm of Divine Essence, one does not go beyond the Oneness of All-Being. Whether attribute or essence, whether form or formlessness, all issue forth from that one radiance which, because of its infinite power, assumes the duality of the beloved and the lover, of the knowledge and the knower, of the lord and the servant, of the creator and the creation. Whoever makes an absolute distinction where it is all absolute unity may not be counted among the initiated.

Each path, whether linked with one divine form or another or without any form whatsoever, is the path of love. In principle, the path of Essence is superior to the path of attributes. However, if the path of attributes radiates with love and the path of Essence only with knowledge, then the former becomes superior to the latter. Gul Hasan recalls an occasion one night when Ghauth Ali Shah asked one of the fellowship to recite that section of Rumi's *Mathnawi* which related the story of Moses and the shepherd boy:

One night, Moses on his way to Sinai came across a lonely shepherd and was astonished at the way he was expressing his love for God. There he was under the canopy of the stars sitting by himself talking to his Creator as if he were his friend and beloved: "O God! How long have I searched for You, I would make you rest on my lap, comb your hair, and place before you all that I have." He was expressing his love as if he were talking to someone who had a form and a body. Moses was shocked at this kind of devotion and interrupted to admonish the poor shepherd, reminding him that God was far above such description and address.

Having silenced the shepherd and pleased with himself that he had given him an appropriate lesson in theology, Moses ascended the sacred mountain where he heard a Voice saying, "Moses! What have you done to that shepherd boy? Why did you interrupt him while he was talking to Us? Why did you separate my servant from Me? You were sent to humanity to bring them closer to Me, not to widen the gulf between Me and My creation."

Gul Hasan reports that, as this story was being read that night, they all saw, for the first time in their eighteen-year association, Ghauth Ali Shah so deeply touched that tears started rolling down his face and everyone in the company was in tears. How can one speculate as to the state of his heart when he wept at the story of a simple shepherd boy and his love for God? The incident encapsulates the secret of Ghauth Ali Shah's life and teaching. Love of God is a mystery between the lover and the beloved. In whichever form or ritual, in whichever temple or mosque that love is manifested, nobody can dare say a word or raise any theological objection. The incident that night in that fellowship also encapsulates the hermeneutic challenge of the Indian subcontinent. Is it for Muslims or Hindus to judge each other's modes of worship and devotion? The story which Rumi narrates in such a simple and heart-rending manner reminds us that the Indian people and, for that matter, the world at large can join hearts in real gnosis and love, and save ourselves from many a tragedy enacted in the name of religion. I believe that Ghauth Ali Shah wept that night at the recital of that story not only because it was a story of love between humanity and God but also because he could see through the eye of his heart into the future of his country; how his countrypeople, both Hindus and Muslims, would fail and fail utterly to live up to the challenge of transcending the diversity and the opposition of their religious symbols for the sake of the Unity of All-Being.

Stories

Ghauth Ali Shah taught through both discourses and stories. However, he preferred stories to scholarship. He was aware that, unless the heart was open, no new knowledge would take root. First one must wake up, then one can truly learn. Most stories are intended to awaken the novice and allow him or her to see self and the world in a different light. This objective is sometimes achieved by registering a shock or by presenting a riddle. As one unravels the riddle, one unties the knot of one's own self. Some stories might appear contrary to common sense, natural laws and logical expectations. All, however, have one unmistakable effect, namely that they raise the level of our consciousness even when we may regard them as irrational and nonsensical. The outer narrative may conceal, fold within fold, many meanings. It is left to the recipient of the story to reach for its depths.

It is not only our reason that reads the story but also our soul. The outer mind has sometimes no clue as to how the inner mind is receiving the message. A story with an esoteric intention is addressed to the inner person. The outer person is a mere bystander. It seems that the stories are the details of what the soul already knows after her supra-rational mode.

Though each story is unique, it shares with the rest of its kind a special language which works through allegory, metaphor and symbol. For instance, a mirror is a metaphor for emptiness, and a symbol for consciousness and also for the heart. A diamond is a symbol for the potential of self-development; and a cup represents expectation and yearning, and also personalized gnosis. There are also certain symbolic figures. An esoteric meaning is superimposed upon their traditional meanings. For instance, Moses represents outer knowledge, whereas Solomon represents the inner. When love is mentioned, it symbolizes a state in which ego has been transcended and all otherness has been set aside.

A story also has an initiatory role. The initiation takes place, first, at the psychic level by creating a state of mind which one has not experienced before. Some stories lead to a crisis at this psychic level. The sense of crisis may be expressed in terms of either rejecting the story as sheer nonsense or laughing at its obviously hilarious and uncanny character. But irrespective of one's conscious response, we are not the same person as before we knew the story. Second, the initiation goes beyond the psychic level by arousing in the novice a latent faculty, namely the ability to look at the world as a symbol of one's inner reality. The third and final step in the initiatory process involves the storyteller who represents the guide, or the master who completes the process of initiation by interpreting the story and unveiling its mystery. There are several stories which stress the principle of gradual initiation, though it is also true that some may be transformed by one glance of an awakened soul or through some simple act of charity and love. In the actual encounter between two spiritually sensitive individuals, it is difficult to say who initiates whom.

There are stories about strange men, the mad ones, the *majzubs*, those who are absorbed in their inner states to such a degree that they have lost contact with the outer reality. Madness is sacred in the Orient. Whether madness is due to total indrawing of reason or is a device on the part of some to conceal their real status, it is difficult to tell. In the stories these mad ones appear like children, funny and yet powerful. They confuse and frighten, but also they challenge and awaken the humble and the sincere who reach for them. Though gentle at heart, some of them are at times as wild as a whirlwind. They seem to occupy the extreme end of poverty, bereft of even their reason and ego.

There are stories which refer to powers manifested by certain masters and rishis; powers of their imagination and will, and powers of their recital of the sacred invocations, particularly the Islamic recital of negation and affirmation "There is no god but God", as if the entire journey from the divine attributes to the Divine Essence is a journey of power. We are also warned that the seeker should not stay at the stations of power but go beyond them. The quest is not for power but for gnosis and vision of the Ultimate Reality.

Before each traveller, three paths are always open: through cosmos, through self and beyond both. Most stories are focused on the second journey, from one's ego to one's soul. It is on this inner path that the traveller meets strange people, hears strange stories and sees strange things. It is on this journey that both the illusion and the meaning of time may be shown to us. It is on this path that we leave body behind and look at our soul as a reality apart and impassive. There we witness the sources of those powers which extraordinary men and women manifest in the world below. There we are led to have the first taste of real gnosis of how the soul of all the souls is both one and many at the same time, and how its levels of manifestation vary from person to person, from one station of gnosis to another, from one living body to another living body. When we re-enter the world, returning from this inner journey, we have many stories to tell. Those who listen carefully know that each story is their own story, whether it be of Ulysses or of Sindbad.

Discourse is addressed to our intellect, whereas a story is addressed to our entire being. It is better if one gives a story to interpret a story. If one interprets a story discursively, then one replaces the story by discourse as though destroying a knowledge that was a living being in the form of a story. Hence, I present the stories as narrated by Gul Hasan and Ghauth Ali Shah without further comment on their mysteries and meanings. Now it is your journey through these stories, from one form after another to the Formless One who is "everywhere and yet nowhere".

Hasan Askari

About Sufism

As Islam spread out from seventh-century Arabia into Egypt, Syria and Mesopotamia, and thence across Asia to India and Indonesia and from North Africa to Spain, much of its history was characterized by tolerant and lively exchange and debate with other faiths and philosophies – Zoroastrianism, Eastern and Western Christianity, Judaism, the Greek classical tradition, Buddhism, Jainism and Vedanta (Hinduism). Even where encounters took the form of conflict and bloodshed, cross-fertilization of religious ideas occurred. The purity and simplicity of Islamic belief in the omnipotence and unity of One God was enriched, deepened and at times overwhelmed by extra-Islamic metaphysical and esoteric dimensions.

At the same time as it participated in intense religious, philosophical, cultural and scientific cross-fertilization that changed the world, the Islamic empire was also a political entity. For over six centuries after the death of the Prophet, it established a religio-political system under a *caliph*, the leader of the Islamic community. The tensions between worldly ambitions and spiritual life showed themselves in the mid-seventh century in the murders that inaugurated the caliphate of the Umayyad kinsmen, once opponents of the Prophet. From very early in the Umayyad rule there were reactions from the faithful against their decadence and secularization of the faith, but it was in the eighth century when the Umayyads ruled an empire stretching across Arabia, Egypt, Syria, Iraq and much of Persia that the tension between the political and religious elements of Islamic civilization prompted a protest that was to take lasting form. While the Umayyads lived a life of ostentatious luxury and worldly power, pious men began adopting a simple life of material poverty coupled with a striving toward mystical knowledge of God. The movement rippled out to Syria and to Persia and eventually to North Africa and India. Its adherents became known as *Sufis*, "wearers of wool"; i.e. of poor garments.

Sufism derived its inspiration from the Qur'anic idea of *zikr*, voluntary remembrance of God's presence in the world and in one's self. In addition to the canonical obligations of worship and prayer, these Muslims laid the foundations of voluntary practices of God-remembrance which later became more formalized under one mystical order or another. Early on, Islamic thought, both philosophical and mystical, was influenced by Greek philosophy in general and by the Neoplatonic doctrines in particular. Without forsaking the Qur'anic insistence on the transcendent Oneness of God, Sufism embraced ideas such as the unity of all being (*wahdatul wujud*) represented by Ibn Arabi (d. 1240 CE), and the union of the human soul with her divine source, a theme which recurs in the poetic works of Rumi (d. 1273).

But for many Muslims, the idea of union with God was tantamount to *shirk*, the association of another being with the Unity of the Divinity, considered the greatest sin of all. In 922 CE the Sufi Al-Hallaj, who said "I am the Truth", was crucified for blasphemy, and yet Hallaj soon became one of the greatest influences in the mystical life of Islam. His utterance about his identity with the Divine Essence came to be regarded as a *shatha*, a word uttered in a state when one is beside oneself, when one no longer exists in a mystical state but God alone exists.

But it was the voice of Al-Ghazali (d. 1111), the greatest Islamic theologian, which was key to the acceptance of Sufism in the general religious life of Islam. Al-Ghazali's scholarly and religious life began in Baghdad immersed in the philosophical dialectic between faith and reason which had pre-occupied Islamic thought for centuries. This led him into a crisis of faith and from there to mysticism.

> I realized with certainty that it is the mystics above all others who are on God's path. ... How must one follow this mystic path? Purity (*tazkia*), the first condition, means complete purification of

the heart from everything but God (to whom be praise). The key thereto, and also the password of the ritual prayer is to sink one's heart in the contemplation of God; its goal is complete identification with God.[1]

This is how Ghazali resolved the tension between identification with the Divine Unity and the Qur'anic requirement of purity of heart. His writings affirming both the Qur'anic truth and the truth of the mystical experience were a major factor in establishing Sufism within Islamic orthodoxy.

The first Islamic contact with India took place when the Arabs conquered Sind at the beginning of the eighth century, and from the twelfth century onwards Islam spread into North India and within a few decades an extensive engagement began between Islam and the complex Indian cultural and spiritual tradition. In India, the Sufis found an occult metaphysical dimension very close to the Islamic sense of Divine Unity. A silent consensus of spirit developed between the Sufi masters and Hindu *rishis*. Dara Shikoh, the Mughal prince (d. 1657, the eldest son of the Emperor Shajahan who built the Taj Mahal), translated the Upanishads into Persian and went to the extent of saying categorically that the difference between Sufism and Vedanta was only linguistic!

The convergence of the Vedantic and Sufi ideas created an eclectic civilization which survives, despite several ideological reversals, in Indian art and music, in architecture and language. The medieval boom of the Bhakti tradition (devotional and theistic Hinduism) and the emergence of Sikhism owe much to the Vedanta-Sufi confluence. For itself, Sufism received many meditative techniques from the Vedantic and Buddhist traditions. But however it was influenced, Sufism retained its Islamic identity, its simplicity in matters of faith and worship, and its hospitality to all humanity. With profound and positive enrichment on both sides, there also emerged in the Indian

[1] A. Hottinger, *The Arabs*, London, 1963; 94.

Sufi fold many superstitious and pantheistic ideas which were responsible for the rejection of Sufism in general by certain Muslim puritanical reformers.

The contemporary Indian Sufi scene involves a network of Sufi shrines linked with the Sufi orders that became an integral part of the life of both the elect and the masses. The most important Sufi shrine is that of Muinuddin Chisti (d. 1236) in Ajmer in north-east India. The Chistiya Order which he founded is the most eclectic and popular order. The other popular, but more pietistic and esoteric, order is the Qadriya, founded by Abdul Qadir Jilani (d. 1166). It was one of the Qadriya masters, Mian Mir, who was approached by Guru Arjan, the fifth Sikh Guru, in the late sixteenth century to lay the foundation of the Harimandir (now the Golden Temple). Such was the connection between the Sufi and early Sikh piety. The other two major orders in India, but with smaller followings than the Chistiya and Qadirya, are Suharwardiya, founded by the Persian master Abu Najib Suharwardi (d. 1168), and Naqshbandiya, founded by Bhahuddin Naqshband (d. 1390).

Sufi tradition in India continues to hold the torch of hope for spiritual rapport between Muslims and Hindus. Its ability to create an eclectic culture as it did in medieval India remains as strong and relevant in the fast-growing technological society of today.

Hasan Askari

Translator's Note

The present work is a selective reorganization of the original text, maintaining its overall ambience and sentiment. The order of the material in the translation as it relates to the original edition of 1898 is listed on pp. 213–15.

We have avoided translating frequent citations of Urdu and Persian poetry, as their rendering in English would have lost their beauty and eloquence as well as affecting the form and symmetry of the present work.

Where explanations of the Arabic and other terms are not found in the text, they are listed in the glossary.

Quotations from the Qur'an are italicized and followed by chapter and verse number.

SOLOMON'S RING

INTRODUCTION

What is praise and what is thankfulness? Who is the praisegiver and who is the one being praised? Who is giving thanks? Who is the one to whom these thanks are offered?

If the drop is reality then the ocean is lost and if the ocean is reality then the drop is non-existent. So long as one concentrates on a grain of sand the sun is hidden from one's view, and as soon as the sun emerges before one's eyes the grain is no longer in sight. Both the drop and the ocean, both the grain and the sun are relative. In every drop an ocean is surging. Every grain owes its existence to the sun and every sun owes its existence to the grain. So also, every river owes its being to the drop; and in the drop one sees an ocean. But, there is neither drop nor ocean, nor grain nor sun. Everything is nothing.

If one thing is rare, another has no sign nor locality. Whatever "is" is above both speech and script, outside all understanding and comprehension. Whatever is comprehended is wrong. Whatever is written is insanity. So, that which is "so" is above all attribution. No; no virtue and error, reward and punishment, separation and union, conjecture and speculation, remembrance and forgetfulness, obedience and rebellion – all are acceptable. All is an offering, all reliable, all reasonable. When there is neither oneness nor twoness then there is nothing but "suchness". *Everything perishes except His face* [Q. 55.27]. Where then is there room for speculation or for any conjecture whatsoever? It is one's own praise, one's own appraisal, one's own story, one's own statement, one's own utterance, one's own state. One is both the thanksgiver and the recipient of thanks. One is both the remembered and the one who remembers. The ocean is lost in the drop and the drop is annihilated in the ocean. The sun covers the grain and over the sun the grain is overpowering. There is a tree hidden in the seed and in the tree the seed appears from nowhere. In being there is witnessing and in witnessing there is being. *He is the first and the last, the hidden and the manifest* [Q. 57.3]. He is in my heart and my heart is in His hand. As the mirror is in my hand so I am in the mirror. Neither separation nor union, neither contact nor elaboration, neither oneness nor twoness, neither I-ness nor you-ness. Neither is testimony beneficial nor denial harmful. There is no other to bear the secret or to confide in, neither good nor evil, neither desire nor concern. If "this" is right, "that" too is valid, free from all determination and limitation. Neither losing remembrance nor losing forgetfulness; there is neither barrier nor obstacle; neither count nor number. *Say: God. He is One and He is transcendent* [Q. 112.1].

There is no distinction between the name and the named. Word and meaning are not two separate things. Whether you call it essence or attribute it is one and the same. If there is any, then He is; if there is nothing, then there is nothing. There is neither Adam nor Satan in the entire cosmos, neither Solomon nor Sheba in the whole kingdom. He is the whole word and He is the meaning and He is the One who is the magnet for all hearts. You cannot see the sun but with the help of the sun. Only when the light of the sun fills one's eyes can one see the sun. He is Himself the veil, Himself the screen, Himself the light and Himself the sun. And the sun is hidden inside the light and the sun is itself all-light. Himself the seer and the seen; Himself the witness and the sight; Himself the speech and

Himself the speaker. *He is One. There is no god but He* [Q. 5.73]. The seer and the seen and the seeing are All One. I am now bewildered – of what account is my own perception?

If there is praise there is no sign of the other; if there is gratitude there is no trace of obligation. Himself the hearer and Himself the seer; Himself the word and Himself the speaker. Whatever He wishes He says and He does. Who does then really say? Who does then really act? *When you threw what you threw, it was God who threw* [Q. 8.17].

The praise is essentially one with the praiseworthy; thanksgiving one with the recipient of thanks. As one single wave rises from eternity, a host of temporal worlds appear on our horizon. The appearance of Being is the vision of Beyond-Being. There is an ecstasy of the multiplicity with respect to Unity. Reality is one with metaphor; praise and blame move in one step; colour and colourlessness join in one form, one meaning and one procession. There is neither complaint nor protest.

O my Lord, You have not created all this in vain [Q. 3.191].

From essence, attributes; from attributes, acts; from perfection, imperfection; from imperfection, perfection, continuously emerge and persist. From the named, the name; from the soul, the body; from the height, the depth, continuously emerge and persist. *Why don't they look into their own selves?* [Q. 32.27].

Beauty has no rest; she is restless behind the veil. Goodness overflows towards expression. The beloved has torn her veil and the lover has no strength to bear the vision. Beauty without illumination, and the seeker in a state of rest are impossible. The beauty of essence put on the garment of attributes. One who is colourless appeared in colours and forms. It is that which is the beginning which is the first wave: that is the emanation; that is the descent; that is the first grade; that is the last grandeur. Whatever state, whatever utterance, whatever description, whatever hint one may offer – all are relative – whether expression or illumination, whether summary or detail, whether revolution or change, whether image or fancy, whether personification or limitation, time and creation, cosmos and chaos – all sprang from the Prophet's hadith: "What God created first was my light".

The intended purposes which precede in knowledge are later in manifestation. Before the seed is spread the fruit is kept in view, then the tree is manifested. Branch and leaf, fruit and flower are the details of the divine summary. The ultimate purpose is to manifest the fruit. The seed hidden in the fruit and the tree hidden in the seed. The hidden in the manifest and the manifest in the hidden; unseen in the seen and seen in the unseen; inner in outer and outer in inner – all are there, and hence the Qur'anic verse: *He is the first and the last, the hidden and the manifest* [Q. 57.3].

Within the form of the worshipped is the meaning of One who is worshipped. Within the form of one who prostrates is One to whom that prostration is directed. Within the *shariah* of Ahmed (law of the Prophet) is the reality of *Ahad* (Oneness). Himself the revelation and himself the inspiration; Himself the prayer and Himself the peace; Himself the messenger and Himself the message; Himself the Sender and Himself the One to whom it is sent. Neither I nor You; neither speech nor utterance; neither sight nor listener; neither far nor near. *He is nearer to you than your jugular vein* [Q. 50.16].

Neither is there the outer as distinct from the inner path, nor is the truth of unity different from its reality. Himself the circumference; Himself the compass; Himself the centre; Himself the axis; Himself the knowledge; Himself the will. He is the beginning and He is the end; all-pervading; all-subsisting. He is all the traces and He is all the modes. He is the jug and He is the cup. He is the wine and He is the wine-house. By Him all the oceans rise and fall. The bubble and the wave borrow from His light. His grandeur knows neither why nor wherefore.

Without hesitation and without concern a light appeared from behind the veil of the mysteries, which took the form of the presence, the direction and the K'aba, the celestial king, the high soaring eagle, a gallant river in the expedition into the wilderness of abstract truth. The crowned prince of the realm of Unity; the knight of the tournament of individuation; a daring gnostic; the perfection of the perfected; the veil of the veils united without veil; witness without obstacle; a sun of Reality; a bridge between Beyond-Being and being; the renouncer of everything except Unity; the burner of the two worlds; the light of fellowship; the great nomad; the destroyer of houses; the individual of the individuals – Sayyid Ghauth Ali Shah Qalander Qadri – emerged on the throne of instruction and speech.

The writer [Gul Hasan] – homeless, intoxicated with the cup of initiation, sometimes roaming the habitats of humanity and sometimes wandering in the deserts; sometimes placing his head on the threshold of the shrines of the elevated ones – was burning for so long with a fire of love in his heart.

During my discipleship, every day I was blessed with the grace of conversation with my lord, biding my time kissing the margins of his courtyard; always present at the open sessions when his light was spread far and wide, and grateful for being permitted into a special companionship and given the opportunity of seeing his vision day and night. It was a state of endless ecstasy, and in that state of constant connection and union I would not have cared to write about my master, nor had I the intellect to set down his teachings, and above all that my lord did not have any love for writing or editing texts. All the time before our eyes there was a world without name or sign. Our natures were liberated from all obedience and imitation. Secrets were revealed; many mysteries were unveiled; and he also gave practical guidance and direction to those who came to him. Some friends in that elect fellowship asked his permission to commit a few of his teachings to writing, but he seemed reluctant. Whatever he did by way of teaching he always wiped, both the first and the last impressions he made upon us. However, during the last days of his life he gave me permission to note down a few things including poetry and stories and I continued to record them for the purpose of my own later recollection. Besides these things nothing else was committed to writing, only to our ears and hearts.

When the eagle of the dome of divinity, the sun of the world of transcendence lifted the veil of manifestation from the face of the Sightless Being, then my restless heart was agitated and whenever I recalled that time of friendship, of joy and happiness I had spent with him, then my distress became unbearable. I could not find anything to occupy myself with except to spend the rest of my life in recollection of the intimacy and union of that vision of beauty and perfection. All my friends agreed with this idea and so supported my broken heart with their trust and expectation that I inevitably lifted my pen and set aside the sorrow of separation from my beloved lord and master.

I had suffered much during those days, sometimes overpowered by a sense of self-abnegation and sometimes by forgetfulness. But, when I turned my thoughts towards recollection of those states and experiences which I had undergone in the company of my lord and master, then, from a world unseen and unbidden, those words spoken by him so long ago emerged with a light of their own before the eye of my heart. As soon as I was able to recall one small detail the entire story leaped before me as if I were hearing it once again. Then he was there, and his utterances, both the speaker and the speech, his face and our ears – then the house of thought echoed with his voice. Whatever I could recall, I committed to writing.

However, there were several things which we heard which are no longer imprinted upon our heart and mind. There were many incidents and situations, day in and day out, when people from different directions and lands used to visit him, placing before him their difficulties and ordeals, and, through his generous attention and graceful breath, each received one or other fulfilment of their purposes or needs. During all these comings and goings, strange powers and miracles were manifested. I have not included those things in this book because my master and lord neither attributed those things to himself nor regarded them as worthy of reference, recollection or appreciation. He always considered every unveiling and every miracle as infinitely inferior to the ecstasy of the state of Unity, and regarded purity of heart as the work of God alone, and this was his real and ultimate intention.

I, Gul Hasan, am a humble servant of the *faqir*. I am neither an expert on Urdu nor do I belong to this country; a wanderer without country and without home and shelter. My country is neither Egypt nor Iraq nor Syria. My country is a city which has no name. My words and my diction are free from poetic intention and I therefore beg my readers to overlook any mistakes of language and expression and concentrate upon the substance and the meaning of what is offered here. This *tadhkira* [record; memoir] I have named *Tadhkira Ghauthya: The Tree of Gnosis*.[1]

> *Gul Hasan*
> *14 Shaban 1301 Hijna [9 June 1884]*
> *Panipat, India*

---

[1] This English translation of the book takes its title from one of the stories because the original title is replicated in another book currently in print.

PART ONE

Stories

1

The Gift of the Mirror

One day he said

Afriend from the days of childhood visited Joseph when he was in Egypt. Joseph asked him whether he had brought anything for him from his native land. "There was nothing", he replied, "that I could think of to bring you as a present that is worthy of your being, except your own self." As he said this, he placed before Joseph a shining mirror of great elegance and beauty.

On the Day of Encounter with God, each one of us will be asked what we have brought as a gift to our Lord and Creator. What is there from one end of creation to the other that can be raised as a gift to the Creator of all things? What flowers from which garden, what art from which artisan, and what ornament from which gold mine can be placed in the hands of One who made and adorned them all? What can be raised as a present to the Lord of Being except the polished mirror of one's heart cleansed of all duality, shining by the light of unity, made elegant by mixing awe with fascination at the prospect of that beauty which surpasses all witnessing? Hence the Qur'anic reminder: *On that Day nothing from one's wealth or family will benefit anyone before God except a heart, pure and gentle* [Q. 26.89].

2

Moses and the Lizard

One day he said

Awealthy noble of the city came to see me. Not long afterwards, a very poor man with dirty, dishevelled clothes entered my room and sat beside the nobleman. The rich man extricated himself from the immediate vicinity of that poor wretch and sat down. When I saw this I remembered a story:

Once Moses was sitting in a house when a lizard scuttling across the roof urinated and a few drops fell on to Moses. Irritated, Moses raised his hands to God and said, "For what purpose did you create that creature?"

God replied, "Moses, do you know that every day this lizard asks me, 'Why did you create that man and what is his purpose?'"

3

Emperor Jehangir and the Majzub

One day he said

The Emperor Jehangir felt a great curiosity to meet the majzub Shah Husayn Dada. The majzub used to sit on a wooden horse to which small wheels were attached and the children in the street would roll the horse hither and thither. It was in this childlike state that he lived his life. The emperor's courtiers advised him not to go in search of the majzub and meet him publicly because it would be beneath his royal station to seek the audience of such a clown.

However, one evening the majzub was passing under one of the balconies of the royal palace. A courtier ran to the emperor and informed him that the majzub was directly beneath his balcony. The emperor ordered that he be hoisted up.

As soon as the majzub was before him, the emperor asked, "How did you find God?"

The majzub replied, "In the same way I found you."

The emperor then asked, "And how did you find me?" to which the majzub responded, "In the same way I found God."

The emperor said, "O madman, I cannot unravel this puzzle."

"Listen, emperor," began the majzub, "had I wanted to meet you, I would have had to first approach the guards of the palace, then their officers, then the courtiers and then their ministers. Indeed, I would have had to plead with all of them for an audience.

Then, that granted, I would have had to appear at an appointed hour in clean clothes that befitted the occasion. Even then I could not be sure that you would even so much as glance at me, let alone meet me. But when you yourself wanted to meet me, you pulled me up without any mediation taking place and without others knowing your purpose or intention."

There are two types of seekers. Those who go from stage to stage and those who are suddenly pulled upwards by a hand from the unseen.

4

The Four Travellers

One day he said

Once there were four travellers passing through a dense forest. When they stopped to rest for the night, because of the dangers from highwaymen, robbers and wild animals they decided they should keep a watch for each part of the night.

The first watch was given to the wood sculptor. While he was sitting alone, his three companions sleeping, he took a piece of wood and began to carve. During his watch in the first quarter of the night he carved the figure of a beautiful woman. Then he woke one of his companions, a dressmaker, to take over the watch while he slept. Noticing what his friend had created and admiring his skill, the dressmaker decided to spend the time of his watch making a beautiful garment for her. After he had made the garment and dressed the statue, it was time to wake up the third watch of the night, who happened to be a jeweller. This man decided to adorn the girl with beautiful jewellery from earrings to necklace, from bracelets to a beautiful belt for her waist.

Now the last watch of the night was about to begin. The jeweller managed to wake the fourth man who was very fast asleep, a good-for-nothing fellow with no skills or arts to speak of. The man rubbed his eyes to shake off his sleep and looked around in the pitch darkness broken only by the last embers of the fire which they had lit when they settled down. In the light of that fading fire he saw to his utter amazement the figure of a beautiful woman, dressed and adorned. He looked at his three friends, now fast asleep, and just admired their skills. He was perplexed because they had left nothing for him to add, and, even if they had, he was unable to offer anything. So he felt very distressed at himself and how useless his life had been and was ashamed before these strangers whom he had met on the journey. The night was quickly receding as he rose with tears in his eyes and did the necessary ablutions to offer a special prayer. There he sat in that still land before sunrise and raised his hands to pray:

"Oh, Almighty and Merciful Lord, give from your boundless mercy a little portion so that I may not be ashamed before these friends as this day rises. You are the Giver of Life, who gives life to everything in the universe, You are all-living and eternal, bestow upon this figure the gift of life, which is in Your power alone to give."

As the first ray of the sun spread across the heavens, a world enveloped in the oneness of the dark sprang into countless forms and images, each claiming separate identity and attention. At that moment of daybreak, there was movement in the figure and there she was, a breathing beautiful woman. So when the travellers awoke, their eyes were filled, not only with the light of the rising sun, but also by the beauty of a living form before them whose miracle confounded them. They could not believe that a form carved out of dead wood could breathe and move.

But she was there, a form among the forms of this world claiming their wonder and admiration. But soon their bewilderment was replaced by mutual hostility as to who had greater claim over her. Each one talked about his contribution to her making, and the fool about his prayers. They had slept the previous night as friends but when they awoke the following morning they became bitter enemies.

However, they agreed on one thing, that they should go into the city and present their case before the magistrate. This they did and the magistrate was baffled by the intensity with which each one of them stressed his part of the story. What mystified him most was the fact that the girl did not utter a single word, as if she were deaf and mute. Finally, he brought the men before the king, hoping that in his presence at least one of them would speak the truth. But each repeated the same story, which was obviously so unbelievable that the king was also greatly puzzled. One of the princes suggested that they should invite a faqir to advise on this inscrutable dispute.

On his arrival, the faqir looked at the assembly and the helplessness of everyone there with the single exception of the mysterious girl who stood amidst them as if she were all alone. Then the faqir led them out of the city and brought them before an old and mighty tree known in ancient times as the Tree of the Oracle. As the faqir asked the tree on behalf of the king for the solution to the mystery, an opening appeared in its trunk. They all watched as the girl walked towards the tree, stepped into the opening and disappeared inside the tree.

So from formlessness emerged the form and to formlessness it returned. *We are of God, and unto God we return* [Q. 2.156].

Such is the case, Ghauth Ali Shah said, with all of us. As soon as we step into this world, we are surrounded by claimants of various kinds and powers – parents claiming us because they brought us up; teachers claiming us because they gave us education; relatives claiming us because they are our kin; friends claiming us because they gave us their love; and rulers and employers claiming that they gave us security and livelihood; and, if we happen to be Muslim, the *imams* claim that we owe them our obedience; and if we happen to be Hindu, then the pandits claim us because they have prayed for us in the temple.

But a day shall come when these relationships and the claims that build upon them will be all nullified, and none shall ever know from whence we came and whither we went. On that day, each soul shall have much to worry about herself. *On that day shall a man flee from his own brother, and from his mother and father, and from his wife and children* [Q. 80.34–6].

5

The Dream of the Raja

One day he said

Think world is transitory, without permanence, a fiction and a dream. He then told us this story.

There was once a raja who, quite suddenly one afternoon, was overcome by hunger. He asked his servants to prepare some food as quickly as possible.

While the food was being prepared the raja fell asleep and dreamed that he had gone hunting with his courtiers and royal guards. He sighted a deer leaping across a clearing in the forest so he galloped after it, losing contact with his entourage in the pursuit.

After a long chase he captured the deer and was about to turn back when he was overcome by thirst. As he searched for water, he came to a well at the edge of a village. A young girl was drawing water and when the raja asked for some she cupped the water in her hands and gave him a drink.

The raja asked, "And who are you?"

She said, "I am a sweeper's daughter."

The raja was immediately distressed because the girl was so low caste and followed her as she walked away carrying the jar of water on her head. When they reached her home and family, the raja began to lament that he had violated the rules of his caste. He asked the family to admit him to their caste by marrying him to their daughter.

The raja then lived with those people and became a street-sweeper himself. He remained there twelve years and fathered several children. Then one day, he fell ill and, in spite of every attention, he passed away.

As soon as he died there, he woke up in his palace. Startled from his dream, he asked his courtiers, "How long did I sleep?"

They replied, "Just a few moments ago you asked us to prepare food. The food is nearly ready so you slept at most a couple of minutes." The raja immediately arose and asked his courtiers to prepare to go hunting.

As he moved about in the forest, he passed through the same situation as in the dream, until he finally reached the sweepers' street where he heard cries of mourning coming from one particular house. The people in that place told him the same story he had seen in the dream and, as he looked at the dead man's corpse, he found he was looking at his own body. He began to wonder who he really was – the one who was lying dead or the one who was alive and looking at the corpse.

Suffice to say that he renounced his kingdom and proceeded to live as a hermit.

6

Jesus and the Power to Raise the Dead

One day he said

There are several stories about Jesus, his disciples and those who remained around him and followed him wherever he went. Among them was a man who was very attracted to the miracle of bringing the dead back to life. Whenever he found Jesus alone, he would plead that he was sincerely anxious to learn the secret of raising the dead; of performing the miracle himself. Jesus tried several times to dissuade him from this obsession, and even warned him that it would be fatal for him. But, like all those whose mind is set on something, he continued to press for it. One day, having received assurance from his follower that he would not test the invocation on anybody, Jesus confided his secret.

On the same day, excited as he was at the extraordinary secret he now possessed, the follower left the city and found in the adjacent forest the skeleton of a tiger. Over the heap of bones, he recited what Jesus had taught him. At once, and to his horror, a living stately tiger sprang to his feet and, as it was hungry, roared at the man and promptly tore him to pieces.

At that time Jesus was returning to the city and passed by the spot where his disciple was being consumed by the tiger. He asked the beast why he killed him. Thereupon, the tiger replied, "He acted as my creator but failed to provide my food."

7

Satan's Plea of Innocence

One day he said

There was a man who was very fond of Satan and somehow earned his confidence. One day he said to Satan, "My friend, I feel really sad that so many people blame you for so much."

Satan replied, "I am not responsible. It is out of enmity towards me that people say what they do. Come, let me show you a strange spectacle."

Satan took the man inside a city and whispered to him, "Today is the day of destruction for this city. Just watch."

Satan and the man entered a shop selling sweetmeats, where Satan then dipped his finger into a vat of honey and wiped the sticky liquid on the wall. Within no time at all hundreds of flies had been attracted to the spot and not long after a lizard appeared in pursuit of the flies. All this activity provoked the sweet vendor's cat which pounced on the lizard just as a soldier and his dog were passing by. The dog became restless at the sight of the cat and jumped at it, which so startled the cat so that it leapt into the vat of honey. This made the sweet vendor so angry that he hit the dog with whatever came to hand and the dog died instantly. The soldier who owned the dog became upset, lost his temper and killed the sweet vendor. Thereupon all the sweet vendors in the street leaped upon the soldier and killed him. When the news of the soldier's death reached his regiment they rushed upon that city and destroyed it.

Satan turned to his companion and said, "Tell me, I ask you, how far was I responsible? The effort was all theirs, yet they make me the target of their blame."

8

Negation and Affirmation

One day he said

One of our friends went into his village mosque one night to offer his prayers. There he saw a man performing zikr [remembrance], eyes closed, chanting the mighty words of negation and affirmation. When he said, "*La Ilaha* [There is no god]", he disappeared, and when he said, "*Il'l'Allah* [but God]", he reappeared.

The following morning, while our friend was standing in the street outside the mosque, he saw a faqir approaching him. "You must have been surprised at what you saw last night," said the faqir, adding as he left, "Be at the mosque tonight and I'll show you something more surprising."

When our friend entered the mosque the following night he saw the faqir already settled in his zikr. When he said the words of negation, he disappeared along with the faqir, and at the recital of affirmation he reappeared with him. During his disappearance he had no idea where he was, nor could he understand how he was reunited with his consciousness as an existence and an identity.

After some time, the faqir stopped his strange zikr and turned towards him, and said, "It is all a great jugglery – even if you reach perfection in the art of zikr you will still have no clue about God. Have you?"

9

The Snake-charmer

One day he said

Once an Englishman was camping in a forest when he came across a large assembly of snake-charmers. Curious, he asked why they had gathered at that particular spot. He was told that there was there an old snake-pit and that the snake to be found in it was not only very large and poisonous but also very unusual. Indeed, its venom was so far-reaching that it was capable of killing not only its immediate victim but also all members of that victim's family irrespective of where they might be. What's more, the snake's breath was so fiery that even the trees were scorched. Although many well-known charmers had come and gone, so far none had been able to hypnotize and capture the creature. Now, these snake-charmers were assembled there to await the guru of snake-charmers from Bengal.

The Englishman was both impressed and amused. He said, "Don't worry. Simply follow my instructions: Gather some dry wood and place it around the perimeter of the snake-pit. Then play your flutes so that the snake will emerge."

They acted accordingly. In time, the mysterious snake rose from the pit and, blowing its fiery breath, ignited the surrounding dry wood which then burned fiercely. The snake moved to and fro in an attempt to escape but was eventually devoured by the flames. Out of fear it was consumed by the very flames it had lit itself.

10

The King and the Four Thieves

One day he said

Sultan Mahumud had a strange habit of wandering in disguise in the city at night. One night it so happened that he passed through a deserted place where he saw four men together. He asked them who they were, to which they replied, "We are thieves."

The disguised sultan said, "That is also my profession. May I join you? Indeed, why shouldn't we all go tonight and break into the royal palace?"

The sultan then enquired after each individual's particular skill.

The first said, "I understand the speech of animals."

The second said, "I can smell where treasure is located."

The third said, "I can open any lock without a key."

And the fourth said, "I recognize anyone I have seen once, even on a dark night."

It was then the sultan's turn to describe his particular skill, whereupon he said, "I have strange powers; if a convict is doomed to be hanged, a single nod of my head will secure his release."

The thieves were impressed and rejoiced at this skill, saying, "With one such as you with us we have nothing to fear." The five men set off towards the royal palace. On the way they came across a dog which barked at them.

The sultan asked, "What does the dog say?"

The one who understood the speech of animals said, "The dog says one of our number is a king."

The sultan asked, "Whom does he point out as the king?"

At that moment the dog stopped barking.

Some time later they entered the royal palace. One of the thieves identified the place where the treasure was hidden; one opened the lock without using a key and, having thus accomplished their purpose, they turned to leave. The sultan also took his leave having first established where he could find them again.

In the morning the news broke of a massive burglary in the palace. The sultan sent his officers to the place the four thieves said he could find them. They were apprehended and brought to the scaffold. The king, however, had instructed his officers that the hanging should not proceed until he sent word for it to so do.

As the four thieves stood by the scaffold they asked one another, "Where is our fifth friend?"

At this moment one of them recalled that the barking dog the night before had told them that one of their number was in fact a king. The fourth thief said, "If I could see our friend now, I would surely recognize him."

So they said to the officer in charge, "We are prepared to hang for our crimes, but we request an audience with the king before we meet our death."

When this was so arranged and they came before the king, the fourth among them said, "Your Majesty, last night we worked our skills very well. Now is the time for you to demonstrate your skill so that we may be freed from this trial."

The king laughed and pardoned them all.

While the gnosis of the king was not with them they were all convicts but, when they achieved gnosis, then their act became the act of the king. Then where is the crime and where is the hanging? All this turmoil is because of duality and self-perception through duality.

11

Kabir's Connection and Disconnection

One day he said

Once Kabir Das [d. 1518] was disentangling some skeins of silk and rearranging them. Someone asked him, "What are you doing?"

He replied, "I disconnect from this side and then connect to the other side."

Then the visitor asked, "What is hovering over your head?"

Kabir Das replied, "Departure!"

The truth is that unless departure hovers over a person's head it is difficult for them to disconnect from one side and connect to the other.

12

The Prophet's Dialogue with Gabriel

One day he said

It is said that when the archangel Gabriel brought the revelation to the Prophet, the Prophet asked him, "Gabriel, do you know from where you received this revelation?"

Thereupon, Gabriel replied, "I can't reach beyond a point in the heaven. At that very point which cannot be surpassed, I hear a voice from the Unseen. My task is to bring that voice to you. Beyond this I know nothing."

The Prophet said, "The next time this voice comes to you, fly over its wings and look and try to reach its source."

Gabriel followed the Prophet's advice. As soon as he heard the voice from the Unseen, he took to his wings and followed it back to its Source and to his utter amazement he saw the Prophet himself speaking that revelation. Then he looked towards the earth and he was further amazed to see that the Prophet was in his place down below.

Commenting upon this, the Qalander said: It does not mean the Prophet was God, but within one indivisible instant the Prophet showed himself to Gabriel in both the worlds.

13

Imam Husayn's Dialogue with Ali

One day he said

When Imam Husayn was twelve years old he asked his father Imam Ali, "Whose love resides in your heart?"

Ali said, "Indeed it is your love."

Then Husayn asked, "And also of my brother Hasan?"

Ali said, "His love also."

Then Husayn asked, "Of my mother too?"

Ali said, "Of your mother as well."

"Of my grandfather?"

"Of course, his love also."

Thereupon Husayn asked, "Of God also?"

"Yes."

Then the child protested: "What sort of heart have you got? Is it a heart or a hotel? In a heart, only one love can reside, not so many."

Then Ali embraced him and said, "My son, you speak the truth."

What Ali taught Husayn is summed up in a few lines of poetry attributed to Ali:

My son, your thought is in you.
That is enough for you.

Your pain and its remedy are inside you.
Everything is included in you.
Nothing is excluded.
You are the source, you are the word, you are the logos.
My son, you appear very small in body
But within you there is a limitless world.

14

Noah and Satan

One day he said

As we all know, after Noah's prayer a great flood came to pass. As Noah entered the ark he was joined by Satan who said, "Good heavens! What an amazing event you have brought about. You prayed and so brought about the destruction of all creation. It seems to me that you became weary of calling them all to guidance whilst I grew disgusted with beseeching them not to turn to you. Now after a long time we can both stretch out comfortably and sleep without any anxiety about either guidance or misguidance."

Because of what Satan said, Noah was unable to cease crying until the day he died.

15

Something in Between

One day he said

Faith lies between fear and hope, as the hadith says. This implies that faith is the third, in the middle; it is neither fear nor hope but something in the middle.

Then he cited the Qur'anic verse: *Indeed the friends of God are those who neither fear nor grieve* [Q. 2.62].

Between belief and disbelief lies the path of poverty.
And practice of poverty is faith.

16

The Story of Hallaj

One day he said

Hallaj [d. 922] was hanged because he added the word *haq* [truth] to *ana* [self].[1] Yet otherwise the whole world says "Haq, Haq" many times and nobody is hanged.

Then somebody asked him [Ghauth Ali Shah], "Is it true that the 'true' servants are found only among Muslims and in no other community?"

Thereupon he said, "Each community believes that adepts are found only among themselves. The fact is that they are found in every community. The grace of God is not limited to any particular group."

---

[1] Hallaj is reported to have said openly *Ana'l Haz* (I am the truth) which became one of the bases of the orthodox charge of blasphemy against him. For details, see Louis Massignon, *Passion d'Al-Hallaj*, vols. 1 and 2 (Paris, 1922), translated as *Tasin* by Abdus Salam (Leeds, 1991).

17

Sultan Mahumud and the Hindu Boy

One day he said

Among the captives Sultan Mahumud Ghaznavi had brought from his exploits in India there was a Hindu boy. For some mysterious reason the sultan showed extraordinary compassion towards the boy and made him stay in his palace. Following the king's attitude, everyone treated the boy with great love and respect. As he grew up in the love and confidence of the sovereign, he was given charge of an important wing of the royal army and had to leave the capital on one of the military exercises.

When the time came to take leave of the emperor, the Hindu boy was in tears. Asked why he was crying, the boy said, "I was recalling the days of my childhood when my mother, at some mischief on my part, used to warn and frighten me that if I did not behave properly Sultan Mahumud would one day come and take me away." The boy paused. The emperor was listening to his tale with great interest.

The boy continued, "As soon as that name was spoken, I used to tremble with fear, whereas now I know how kind and generous the emperor is – how shocked and delighted my mother would be to see me surrounded by the sultan's love and protection."

His mother, unaware of her son's situation with Sultan Mahumud, might have continued to live all her life in distress, a creation of her own fears.

Then I am reminded, Ghauth Ali Shah said, of a *shaikh* who once asked one of his disciples to fetch some fire. But the disciple could not find any fire at that hour. The shaikh shouted, "Go to hell then – there you will find plenty of fire."

So, through no fault of his own, the poor disciple passed through the gates of hell and to his astonishment found that it was all calm and clean, a mere vastness. As he was wondering whether he had come to the right place, he heard a voice: "Here is nothing; anyone who comes here brings their own hell or paradise."

So is the case with us here, said Ghauth Ali Shah. Those who live in a cold climate regard the tropical weather as hell, and likewise those who live in a very hot climate regard the cold of the north as a hell for them. But those who have passed beyond such states of hot and cold are free from changes of environment, seasons and weather. Thus one who has attained the gnosis of the Divine Unity is indifferent to both reward and punishment, heaven and hell. But as soon as one descends from that One Essence to the attributes of God, then one is covered by the attribute of mercy. According to the hadith, God says, "My servant receives Me in the form of his speculation about Me."

Then Ghauth Ali Shah laughed and asked us to consider why people who dishonour another person's religious symbols do not experience remorse or fear of punishment, whereas, if they accidentally dishonour their own sacred objects, they are upset and even punished severely. The reason must be obvious. Each one of them is under the power of their own imagination, of what they hold as sacred and powerful.

But blessed are those who live under the light of their gnosis, their remembrance of the unity of the Divine Essence, above all attributes and differences, for whom all is holy, for whom everything is all things, for whom all is One, and One beyond what they know as such.

The mystery of the Essence and the attributes is similar to the obscure association of soul with body. Ghauth Ali Shah gives an interesting story to shed light on this question.

Once a man went with a blind friend into somebody else's garden full of apple trees. The one who could see climbed on to the blind man's back and then on to his shoulders so as to reach the apples. Seeing the keeper of the garden approaching, he jumped down and ran away, leaving his blind friend to be caught by the approaching keeper.

At this point in the story, Ghauth Ali Shah turned to his friends and asked: Why should the blind man be punished for the crime committed by his friend who was in full possession of his senses? Similarly, why should the body be burnt in hellfire for the soul's acts?

18

Sadness at the Prospect of Death

One day he said

When asked about the nature of sadness at the prospect of death: "Indeed one's heart becomes sad at the moment of leaving a house where one has lived for a couple of years. Our body is a house. All our life here we live in it. To leave it after such a long residence must be really heartbreaking."

Ghauth Ali Shah then recalled one of the Hindu faqirs whom he knew. He had the strange power of transmitting his soul from his body to another body. When Ghauth Ali Shah once asked him how he would feel at the moment of his death, he said, "Well, it is one thing to leave a house by one's own choice, but quite a different thing to be forced to leave."

19

Solomon's Ring

One day he said

It is said that when Solomon lost his ring of power and wisdom he said, "*Al Hamdu 'Lillah* [All praise be to God]." And when he found the ring, then also he said, "*Al Hamdu 'Lillah*." When Solomon was asked about the mystery of uttering the words of praise on such dissimilar occasions, he replied, "The praise was more on the basis of the state of my heart, which was unaltered on both occasions. The heart was neither distressed at its loss nor overjoyed at its recovery."

Solomon's ring was an outer token of inner remembrance and stability.

20

Caliph Harun Rashid

One day he said

Caliph Harun Rashid held a vast festival in Baghdad where thousands of beautiful objects, from artefacts to jewellery to precious stones, were on display. The royal invitation was such that anyone could take anything they wished. So people took what they desired, whatever attracted their mind and eyes and heart.

The caliph had a slave-girl in his harem. She did not pick up anything. She remained quiet. Harun Rashid turned to her and asked, "Why don't you also pick up something?"

The slave-girl said, "Is it true that, whatever one touches in this bazaar of beautiful things, one owns it for life and that thing owns the owner?"

The caliph said, "That is so."

Then the slave-girl placed her hand upon the caliph's hand and said, "Why should I hold a branch when I can reach for the root?"

The caliph said, "As you chose me, so all my kingdom is yours." Thus that slave-girl excelled all the knights and noblemen.

In reality it is a mighty undertaking and choice to give up the branch and reach for the root.

21

Moses on Sinai

One day he said

Once when Moses ascended Sinai he asked to meet a true and special friend of God. The voice said, "There is nobody more special than you, Moses. You are Our special friend." But Moses insisted. The voice said, "Very well, then. Go to that mountain and there you will find a special friend of Ours."

Moses went to the mountain and there he met a man rotten with leprosy and stinking so much that he could not bear to be with him. So he turned back. As he did so the leper shouted, "You came to see me with such enthusiasm, yet now you turn away in disgust."

At this, Moses realized the leper was special but he could not resist asking how it was he came to be in such a frightful state. The leper said, "Lovers live in this condition and are happy with it."

Moses politely asked him, "Do you require anything? Is there anything I can bring you?"

The leper replied, "I had two desires. The first was to meet you and that wish has been fulfilled. The second was that someone should bring me a glass of cool water."

Moses immediately went in search of some cool, clear water but when he returned he discovered a tiger emerging from the leper's cave and the leper himself lying torn to pieces. Moses was saddened by this sight and after burying the man returned to Sinai and asked,

"What was the mystery? Why had he been sent there? Why had all this happened?"

The reply came, "That leper committed two mistakes. First he claimed that he loved Us and yet desired to see another, and second, he should have asked Us to provide him with the water he desired."

There are many among them who do not believe in God unless they join with Him other associates [Q. 27.63].

22

Two Empty Pots

One day he said

The path of *faqiri* [practice of poverty] is something which is whispered in one's ear; then a person who is "there" is brought "here" as if someone had blown on the embers of a fire and a flame leaped forth. In this matter there is no prescribed time, nor prayer, nor fasting, neither any discipline nor exercises. When somebody asked him, "If faqiri is so easy why are disciples made to work so hard?" he told this story:

A man had two empty oil pots which were dirty and greasy inside and out. He went to a man whose job it was to clean pots and asked how long it would take to clean one pot. The pot-cleaner replied, "Forty days."

The man then took the second pot to another pot-cleaner and asked him the same question. This man replied, "Only one day."

Now the first pot-cleaner took great care to scrape the grime from the pot, both inside and out and, having done this, he then heated it gently with a moderate flame. He repeated this process day after day until he was finally able to return the pot to its owner clean and strong.

The second pot-cleaner, however, heaped coals around the pot and then ignited them. This fierce fire cleaned the entire pot in no time at all.

When the two pots were placed side by side, each appeared perfect and clean, but the second pot had become so brittle that it shattered into pieces at the slightest tap. No doubt both pots were clean but while one remained useful the other was now useless.

In this connection he told us another story:

Kwajha Baqi Billah was a master of great concentration. There was a baker who often visited him. On one occasion a few guests arrived at the kwajha's house and he found he had nothing to offer them. The baker, who happened to be visiting the kwajha, immediately went to his bakery to fetch some bread.

The kwajha was very pleased and asked the baker, "Tell me, is there anything you really want?"

The baker said, "Make me exactly as you are."

The kwajha then took the baker inside his chamber and looked at him with such intense attention that the baker became one with the kwajha in form and knowledge. When they came out of the chamber it was difficult to distinguish who was the kwajha and who was the baker. Indeed, the only difference between them was that the kwajha was conscious of his state whereas the baker was not.

After three days the baker died.

The reason the baker died so suddenly was that he had asked for such rapid transformation. This is why sages do not instruct their disciples all at once but insist on prolonged work so that the disciple may progress gradually from one yearning to another.

23

The Pharaoh and the Vial

One day he said

Once the pharaoh lost a precious vial. He called a thousand slaves and said, "Whoever recovers this vial will be generously rewarded and will also be freed." Everybody searched diligently until at last one of them recovered it. All of them appeared before the pharaoh, the one who had found it excited and happy; everybody else sad and distressed.

The pharaoh asked, "Why are they wearing such long faces?"

His minister said, "These are people who were earnest in their quest but unfortunate in not reaching their goal."

Thereupon the pharaoh said, "First give them the reward, then free them."

Then the one who had recovered the lost treasure complained, "Your Majesty, what difference is there then between me and them?"

The pharaoh replied, "As far as we are concerned, there is no difference. You were all the same in your condition as slaves. You were all equal in your earnest search, but what was to be recovered was only one thing, therefore only one could retrieve it. Let us now abolish even that distinction." The pharaoh lifted the precious vial lying before him and smashed it into pieces. "There! All of you are now equal. As far as we are concerned, we were not less by its loss and we are not more by its recovery."

24

Moses and the Leper

One day he said

Once there was a man, wretched and sick, so eaten away with leprosy that he had neither hands nor feet. He was no more than a stinking lump of rotting flesh, yet alive.

It so happened that one day Moses passed by him. The leper pleaded with Moses that when the latter ascended the mountain he should ask God why such a wretch as he had been created.

When Moses raised this question on the mountain the voice said, "Tell him he will be used as a cork for one of the holes in hell."

Moses was baffled by this and felt some trepidation about informing the leper that this was the purpose or reason behind his creation. Nevertheless, it was incumbent upon Moses, on both sides, to return and deliver this message.

With great hesitancy Moses told the leper what had transpired on the mountain. Immediately the leper leaped with joy, saying, "It is enough. I have a purpose and I am in the mind of God." So overwhelmed with happiness was he that he passed away.

25

Shaikh Chilli

One day he said

This world is like the house of Shaikh Chilli; when you throw away the burden then nothing onerous remains.

Once, somebody said to Shaikh Chilli, "This is a pot full of oil. Take it and deliver it to my house and I will give you one rupee."

Shaikh Chilli agreed. As he placed the pot upon his head and started walking he also started thinking: I shall buy a hen out of this one rupee. This hen will give me eggs which I can sell and then I will be able to buy a goat which will produce several kids and in no time at all I will have a herd of goats. I could then sell these and buy a good cow. With the cow's milk I will be able to increase my earnings; I will soon have both a herd of cows and goats and in this prosperity I shall then marry. Then I will have a son. He will learn to walk and soon, whenever I return home, he will run to me and ask, "Baba, Baba, what have you brought for me?" Then I shall become angry with him and say "Go away." He said these last words to himself with such vehemence that the pot of oil slipped from his head and shattered into pieces on the ground. Shaikh Chilli started crying.

The owner of the pot complained, "What have you done? You have broken my pot."

Shaikh Chilli said, "You are concerned only with your pot

whereas the whole world slipped from me as that pot slipped."

If you reflect upon this parable then all the tariqa [gnosis] is fully explained here. That single rupee was that name of God with which a disciple is instructed by the shaikh. From it issue all eggs, chicken, cows and goats. In other words, seekers go through stages, unveilings and miracles, reflections and remembrances, aspirations and ecstasies – all these they need, but when the pot breaks into pieces, all this affair is scattered.

26

Nadir Shah Plunders Delhi

One day he said

It is said that when Nadir Shah invaded Delhi where he staged a massacre and wholesale plunder, one of his chiefs took a beautiful woman from Delhi as his captive. She happened to be the wife of a nobleman whom she loved so dearly that, when she was taken to Kabul and the chief determined to marry her, she pleaded that she was not a widow, her husband might be alive. Why should he not wait six months according to shariah? After that time she would comply with his wishes. "Meanwhile," she said, "give me a house outside the city so that I might watch for the coming of my husband."

After four months her husband came to Kabul in search of her. She told him the story and asked him to obtain her release from captivity. "Think of something to take me away from here." But it was not that easy so she said, "Why not seek the help of a faqir?"

He came across a wandering faqir who said to him, "Why are you wasting your time here in Kabul? There is a great person who lives somewhere in your own city. Go to him, give him my greetings and he will help you."

The distressed lover returned to Delhi and searched for that faqir. Eventually he found him and told him his story. Thereupon the faqir said, "How stupid. Where was the need for him to send you to me when he could have helped you himself? Well, let us see.

Tomorrow is the day of the festival of Holi and we shall stage a passion play. I shall become Krishna and at the point when Radha discovers and joins Krishna, at that moment, you should address me and plead: 'Where is my Radha? She has not reached me'."

So the next day when the festival started and the play began, the faqir was in the guise of Krishna and, as the play progressed, the cry went up, "Radha is lost, Radha is lost." Then, after a time, the cry, "Radha is found, Radha is found."

Then, following his instructions, our lover shouted to the faqir, now in the guise of Krishna, "Where is my Radha, where is my Radha?"

The faqir extended his hand towards Kabul. In the next second that woman was standing in the crowd and the faqir said, "Take your Radha."

When the man asked his wife, "How were you really able to reach Delhi from Kabul?" she replied, "That was the last day of six months. I was distressed and restless and was waiting to see what appeared from the unseen and as I lay down, my eyes closed, I saw in the dream that I had fallen from my bed and when I opened my eyes I was standing amidst a crowd in Delhi. Besides this I do not know what has happened."

27

Sultan Mahumud and the Fishing Boy

One day he said

There was a young boy who went out fishing but failed to make a single catch all day. As evening set in and he sat there sad and distressed, it so happened that Sultan Mahumud passed by on horseback. Seeing the boy sitting alone by the river he approached him and asked him why he looked so sad.

"Nobleman," the boy replied, "we are four fatherless boys and one disabled mother. Whatever fish I catch I carry home and so we somehow save ourselves from starvation."

The sultan replied, "Young man, make me your partner."

The boy agreed. The king then threw the net and by his royal luck caught several fish with one throw. Overwhelmed with joy, the boy turned to the stranger and asked him to take his share. But Sultan Mahumud said, "No, whatever we caught today is all yours. Whatever we catch tomorrow is all mine."

Before leaving the boy, the sultan asked where he lived and the following day instructed his royal guards to bring the boy to the palace. There, before the entire court, he invited the boy to sit on the throne beside him. The courtiers complained and wondered that such a wretched lowly boy should share the sultan's throne. Then the sultan said, "We have accepted this boy and he shall share the kingdom with us."

When people asked the boy what it was in him that had so raised him to this high station, he was himself so bewildered that he was quite unable to answer.

Whoever is picked up by divine love is the Beloved.

28

Shibli Pardons the Criminal Every Time

One day he said

The *caliph* of Baghdad was a disciple of the Sufi sage Shibli. The caliph instructed his officers that, if Shibli demanded the pardon and release of any person convicted and sentenced to death, that person should be reprieved at once.

Once, a dangerous thief was sentenced to death. As he was being taken to be beheaded, Shibli happened to pass by the same way. Shibli enquired about the convict and, having extracted a promise from him that he would mend his ways and desist from any further criminal activity, he asked the officers to release the man.

After a few days the same man was apprehended for an identical crime and was again condemned to death. On hearing this, Shibli once more demanded his pardon and so secured the man's release. In the same manner, the thief came to repeat similar offences and each time Shibli came to his rescue. It appeared that nothing could deter him from a life of crime. Finally he was yet again arrested and sentenced to death. The officers of the court pondered deeply over the matter and concluded that he would never give up his criminal activities and that somehow or other Shibli would always come to his rescue. After these deliberations they decided to take the thief to a remote place unknown to Shibli and where he would be unable to intervene. There they hanged the thief.

When Shibli heard of this, he came to see the corpse. He kissed it, and then addressed it, saying, "Bravo! Bravo! Well done!"

29

The Python and the Faqir

One day he said

There was once, in some distant place, a massive python so gigantic and so dangerous that no one dared walk by that way (out of quite justifiable fear).

One day a faqir was about to go by that same route. People not only warned him but even pleaded with him to reconsider and take another path. The faqir said: "No matter. Let me face whatever may befall me."

When the faqir reached the place where the python was most usually to be found, it puffed out its enormous jaws as if to attack and devour him. The faqir said to the snake, "Be still," and then went on his way. The python lay there quietly.

After a few days the faqir returned and passed by the same place. He discovered the python in a very sorry state. It had grown thin and weak and was lying quite helplessly. The faqir asked, "What is the matter?"

The python replied, "I don't know what has become of me since you last passed this way. People now approach me and tease me and even hit me with sticks. I put up with this but really I am in great distress."

The faqir said, "Poor python, do not practise patience to such a degree or they will kill you. You should at least pretend to frighten the people in order to keep them away from you."

In the same manner, a faqir should not be so sweet that people simply devour him, nor so bitter that they wish to spit him out.

30

The Prince in Rampur

One day he said

A prince was standing on a balcony of his palace when his eyes fell upon his cousin standing on the balcony of her palace nearby. So overcome was he by the sight of her that he immediately fainted. His servant and slave-girls carried him inside the palace and revived him but the arrow of love had pierced his heart so deeply that his health seemed to sink lower and lower each day. One royal physician after another examined him and offered one remedy after another, but all to no avail, for his malady not only persisted but his condition daily deteriorated. Eventually one of the physicians discovered the secret of his ailment and informed the emperor that the prince was smitten with love-sickness. The emperor decided to arrange a marriage between the prince and his cousin, so great preparations and festivities took place for the marriage day.

But the physician who had discovered the cause of the prince's sickness rushed to the emperor and said, "Your Royal Highness, you must postpone the marriage for some more time. Seeing that your son was unable to bear even a single glance of his beloved, how could he possibly survive his union with her? My advice is that you construct two houses separated by a wall with a few transparent windows. The prince and the princess will then live separately yet close. They shall thus see each other by glimpses rather than suddenly and completely."

The emperor agreed to this proposal. The royal couple began to live side by side yet separately in their respective houses. During the course of the days that passed the prince would catch a glimpse of his beloved – sometimes just of her hand; sometimes of her flowing hair; sometimes her eyes; sometimes only a part of her face and sometimes her whole self was captured in a glance: so it went on day after day and the prince not only remained ecstatic at these glimpses but also gradually became more and more accustomed to her beauty and charm. At the end of a long period they were finally married.

The Qalander said that such is the wisdom of a wise shaikh that he brings the novice through gradual unveilings to the threshold of the final vision. Otherwise the suddenness of it all would only destroy the novice.

31

Unveiling the Dead

One day he said

A disciple of Shah Abdul Aziz was very curious about the mysteries of graves and cemeteries. So he came one day and insisted that Shah Abdul Aziz should teach him the zikr of unveiling the dead.

Shah Abdul Aziz gave him the appropriate zikr and asked him to practise it in a cemetery. So he went to the cemetery where Shah Waliullah of Delhi was buried, and performed the zikr. On the first day he was able to see the dead inside their graves. On the second day he saw them sitting inside their graves. On the third day Shah Waliullah looked towards him and said something. A mysterious flame issued from the grave of Shah Waliullah and entered the disciple's body. Under its effect he fell unconscious.

Towards evening on that day Shah Abdul Aziz told his students to go to the cemetery and bring his disciple back. For the next three days and nights the disciple remained in a semi-conscious state and afterwards the disciples used to say that Shah Waliullah's soul always accompanied him and he remained in that state for a year. During that period, there was a stampede in the city because a wild elephant got loose. The disciple happened to be there at the time while people all around him fled in fear. The soul which was with him said to him, "Do not fear." As if this screened him, the charging elephant went right past him as he stood without fear.

32

The Alchemist in Rampur

One day he said

O nce an alchemist came to visit a nobleman of Rampur who entertained his guest for some time. After six months, when the alchemist was thinking of leaving, he said to his host, "I am acquainted with some of the secrets of alchemy and if you would like to learn from me I will gladly teach you."

The nobleman replied, "I do not believe I need them."

The alchemist then said, "So be it. You may not wish to learn the secrets of alchemy from me but at least eat whatever I give you for the next forty days."

The nobleman agreed. As he was about to depart, the alchemist said to the nobleman, "Well, you may not have learned any alchemy from me but I have turned you into an alchemical substance."

With the passing of time, the nobleman's fortunes changed. He lost all his wealth, his home and his family and a time came when he was almost starving. However, he had one small steel cooking pot left and the thought crossed his mind that he should sell it and, with the proceeds, buy some food. Alas, he could not sell it.

It was a hot summer day and the nobleman sat down under a tree and pondered his fate. Had he learned the secrets of alchemy from the man he would now have had occasion to use them. Then immediately he remembered that the alchemist had said that he himself had been transformed into an alchemical substance. So he wiped some of the sweat from his brow and applied it to the cooking pot. As he placed the pot above a fire he had managed to light, it turned into brilliant solid gold. But, at the same time, such a state came over him that he sat there silent and wonderstruck for three days. On the fourth day he disappeared, for his own effect had manifested itself with such terrible suddenness that he was quite unable to sustain it.

33

The Muslim Village

One day he said

There was a village consisting of only Muslim houses. Not a single Hindu dwelling was to be found in that place and consequently whenever Hindus passed by that way there was no place for them to either eat or rest. Some kind-hearted people in the village decided that there should be at least one Hindu home so that any Hindu passer-by could be made welcome. They decided to convert the butcher into a brahmin [the Hindu priest class] and appointed him responsible for the welfare of any Hindu visitors.

One day a brahmin pandit was travelling that way and inevitably decided to stay at the butcher's house. After offering food to the pandit, the wife of the butcher approached the man and said, "Maharaj, I have two sons; one is Ganga Ram [a Hindu name] and other is Kunda Baksh [a Muslim name]. I am baffled as to whether I should first circumcise Kunda Baksh or place the Hindu sacred thread around the neck of Ganga Ram. Whatever advice you care to give me I will follow."

The pandit was both puzzled and surprised, and asked, "What kind of question is that? I don't understand. Perhaps you would elaborate."

The butcher's wife replied, "You see, Kunda Baksh was born when we were butchers and Ganga Ram was born after we became brahmins."

Panditji was nonplussed at this explanation and in total exasperation asked her if she could then tell him whether he should now be buried or cremated.

34

The Letter from the Hakim

One day he said

I received a letter from Hakim Shamsuddin in which the Hakim said he was more disposed towards sin than towards virtue and he sought advice and help in this matter.

Then he [Ghauth Ali Shah] recited the Qur'anic verse: *Where two oceans meet there is a veil between them. In both is reflected the same night* [Q. 55.20]. Then he referred to another verse: *He is the One who makes the night enter day and the day enter night* [Q. 31.29]. Both colours, black and white, are royal colours.

Then he referred to an army camp outside Delhi where a mock battle was being waged as part of a military exercise and discipline. One half of the regiment represented the rebel or enemy and the other half represented forces loyal to the government. Both sides fought an intense battle and eventually the rebel regiment triumphed over the official regiment. Even though the official regiment was defeated and the rebel regiment victorious, it was, in reality, a victory for the government because both the regiments who fought so genuinely against each other were in fact the servants of the same authority. Both received their provisions from the same source – neither group was more favoured than the other – and whether one loses or one wins, the government is neither distressed nor happy. The government was free from either state because on both sides

the game had been played by royal permission. Rebellion and obedience, sin and virtue, good and evil, both were servants under the
same commanding authority. If one is grace another is awe.

Hence, the Qur'anic verse: *We did not create jinn and humanity
except that they should adore their Lord* [Q. 51.56].

Then a man, a disciple, asked, "When all is one, what is reward
and what is punishment? Where is the necessity for heaven and
hell?"

The Qalander said, "They are and they are not. If there is 'otherness', then they are; otherwise they are not. You should face things
in whatever mode you best understand."

35

The Call of the Partridge

One day he said

There were five travellers who were journeying together in great fellowship. One was a cook; one was a drunkard; one was a *hafiz* [one who has memorized the Qur'an]; one was a Sufi and one was a brahmin. They were passing through the jungle and heard the call of a black partridge. One of them asked, "What is it really saying?"

The cook said, "Nothing but onion, garlic and ginger."

The drunkard said, "No, it is saying that every religious jurist is malicious."

The hafiz recited the Qur'an, "When We created the heavens."

The Sufi said, "It is saying, 'Great is His power.'"

And the brahmin said, "Ram, Laxman and Jasrat."

So everyone interpreted the partridge's call after their thought and temperament and nobody knew exactly what the partridge was saying.

36

The Qalander Stays in a Mosque

One day he said

Once we were staying at a mosque in Delhi. There were other faqirs also with us and among them were Baqir Shah and Kambal Posh. Baqir Shah asked Kambal Posh, "Is there any difference in your opinion between *Kufr* and Islam?"

Kambal Posh replied, "Not in the least, because both the branches are official. They are like darkness and light."

Then Baqir Shah asked him, "So on which path do you tread?"

Kambal Posh replied, "On neither. In winter, the sun looks pleasant; in summer the shade is preferable; light in the day and darkness in the night."

Then Baqir Shah turned towards me and asked, "Upon what path do you tread?"

Whereupon I replied, "We join everybody in saying 'There is no god but God and Mohammed is His Messenger.' What and who we are within we have no clue. Some say that within there is God; some believe it is just *nafs* [soul or spirit] joined with Satan. I wonder, if there is God within, how others could survive but, if they survive as servants, then it is understandable."

37

Three Degrees of Certitude

One day he said

Without poverty, to talk about humility is sheer pretence. Without humility, certitude brings about hardness of feelings. Then there is no grace in that certitude. Without grace, certitude is misery.

However, the Qur'an point outs that certitude has three degrees.

Imagine a jug of water before you. Based on the report of someone and also in accord with reason, you have assurance that there is water in the jug. This is the first degree of certitude.

When you lift the lid from the jug and see water with your own eyes, then your assurance is confirmed. This is the second degree of certitude.

When you drink some water from that jug, your knowledge by reason and by vision are united in your experience of the water. This is the third and final degree of certitude. All the veils between you and the object of your knowledge are removed. The reality of the subject and the object is now one. Certitude moves from image to the original reality.

38

Shibli Revives the Carpet Tiger

One day he said

Once Junaid [d. 909] was invited by the caliph to the royal court and Shibli also accompanied him. The caliph spoke so rudely and abruptly to Junaid that Shibli, who was young and excitable by temperament, fell into a rage. With his fist he started pounding the image of a tiger woven into the carpet and at once a living tiger leaped into reality. Junaid saw all this but managed to restore the tiger to no more than the decoration it was on the carpet. The caliph meanwhile persisted in his rudeness and Shibli continued to pound the carpet in fury.

Three times the same miracle occurred, and on the final occasion the caliph himself saw the tiger and started quaking with fear. He came down from his throne and threw himself at the feet of Junaid.

Junaid said, "Forgive this young man, Sire. He did only what his temperament demanded of him as I also did what was necessary." Junaid then recited the Qur'anic verses, *Obey God and His Apostle and those who are in power* [Q. 4.59].

This is how Shibli got his name which means "Baby Tiger" or "Man of the Tiger", although his real name was Abu Bakr. He was Junaid's disciple and also the son of Junaid's sister.

"Obey those in power" means "observe the outward form of the tiger". It may also mean that Shibli was in contact with the archetype and through that contact he was able to give life to the image.

39

Masters, Paths and States

One day he said

The companionship of the master and the disciple ends at the door of gnosis. The disciple enters alone.

The question about the states is not simple. The mystical orders, irrespective of any particular master in a given order, have their separate cultures about mystical states. For instance in the Naqsh-bandiya order incoming knowledge, received with purity of heart, brings about a state of high spirits along with a burning desire or thirst for more knowledge. In the Chishtiya order the novice is given such happiness through the opening of the heart that he is never distressed or exhausted. But in the Qadriya order the novice is left with a growing sense of emptiness, desolation and frustration. Hence, so many in this order lose their courage and give up. But those who persist and remain steadfast experience a sudden implosion as if a trumpet has started blowing inside their soul. Even if the seeker does not attain anything or even if he collapses and dies, there is no remorse because he took the first step towards reality, and the first step towards reality is glorious in itself.

But you should never look at yourself, Ghauth Ali Shah once warned, while you are still a novice, but wait until a proficient comes your way and makes you journey in the realm of your soul.

40

The Power of the Divine Attributes

One day he said

Once a proficient advised one of his disciples to spend time with Bayazid [d. 874]. For a while, the disciple seemed to ignore this advice. When his master insisted, the disciple said that his only aspiration was for a vision of the Divine Essence and he was not interested in witnessing the majesty of the attributes. Nevertheless, his master managed to convince him that by visiting Bayazid he would greatly benefit from another proficient's attention.

However, when the disciple came face to face with Bayazid and when the latter looked at him with a glance that could pierce through both the worlds, the visitor collapsed and soon passed away.

When Ghauth Ali Shah was asked how it was that one who was conversant with Essence was struck down by the light of one attribute, he said that to bear the lights of the attributes was more difficult than to stand the Divine Unity in its Essence. Is it not so that one can look at the sun for some time but not for the same duration at its reflected image in the mirror?

41

The Power of Analogy

One day he said

One of the caliphs was a disciple of Najmuddin Kubra [d. 1220]. As his master lived far away from Baghdad, the caliph wrote to him requesting that someone be sent as his mentor and guide. Najmuddin Kubra sent one of his pupils, a young adept. The caliph liked him and gave him residence in the palace itself, making no distinction between him and the royal household.

In addition to his other charming qualities, the young shaikh was highly creative in giving strange analogies in his religious discourses. For instance, while explaining the relationship between a master and a disciple, he once said: "A perfect master is like a hen. Whatever egg you place under a hen, she will hatch that egg: if it is an eagle's egg, what will issue forth will fly high in the sky; if it were of the hen itself, it will roll in the dust; and if it were of a duck, it will swim in the river." Then he pointed to himself and said as if he were in some state of ecstasy: "We are like ducklings and we swim in the waters of Divine Unity."

When Najmuddin Kubra heard that his disciple and representative had compared him with a hen, he declared, "That idiot will meet his death by drowning."

Unaware that his master had prophesied the manner of his death, the young shaikh continued to enjoy both his popularity in the city and his confidence with the caliph. He could even enter the private parlours of the palace and call upon the caliph without notice or permission. Once it so happened that he lay down on one of the royal couches and went into a deep sleep. The caliph's wife, mistaking the saint for her husband, came and lay beside him and a deep sleep fell upon her as well.

When the caliph entered, he was naturally shocked and upset at what he saw. He turned back in deep agitation. When the shaikh awoke, he too was shocked to see the queen fast asleep beside him. He left the bed carefully and slipped away out of the palace.

In the morning, the caliph ordered that the shaikh be taken out on the river Tigris in a royal boat. Secretly, he instructed the boatmen to sink the boat and drown the shaikh. The caliph's instructions were carried out, and so the shaikh met his end as prophesied by his master.

When the caliph met his wife that night and learned the truth of the situation, he realized what a terrible mistake he had made. He did not know what to do, how to pray for redemption from his evil deed.

He decided to go to Najmuddin Kubra and submit to his judgment. When the caliph came before one of the greatest of the Sufi masters that have ever lived, he placed his royal turban at the saint's feet, and then his sword, and then gold and diamonds. He confessed that he had acted in haste without waiting to know the truth. Gold he had brought as blood money for a life that was wrongly destroyed, and he offered his own sword suggesting thereby that if the blood money were not acceptable he was prepared to be slain by his own sword at the hands of the saint.

At that moment Najmuddin Kubra went into deep meditation. When he opened his eyes and looked at the world around him, he waved aside both the gold and the caliph's sword, and in an unearthly voice spoke so: "The blood of my brother is asking not for one head but for many heads – my head, your head." And then he gave the names, one after another, of all the princes and saints of the Islamic world including that of the illustrious Shaikh Fariduddin Attar [d. 1236]. Then under the same mysterious state of his soul, Najmuddin Kubra began naming one great city after another that would be destroyed. As he was about to say Baghdad, one of the disciples present put his hand upon his mouth. He could only utter the first syllable of the name of the city. So it came to pass that, after destroying all other great cities, when the Mongol hordes entered Baghdad, capital and jewel of Islamic civilization, for some mysterious reason they did not plunder the entire city, as they had done elsewhere. But all those identified by Najmuddin Kubra in his oracle were beheaded by the Mongol sword.

When the Mongol hordes were a few miles away in their march on Nishapur where Attar lived, Attar sat chatting with his friends knowing full well what was in store for the city in a day or two. It is said that he held a cup which he suddenly overturned. Turning to one of his friends, he said, "Now the Mongols have lost the city." He meant that he had veiled the city from the sight of the advancing columns of the Mongol army.

But a hand came from the unseen and held Attar's hand and a voice said, "Not any more. It has been decreed that you will be killed along with others."

"What is my sin?" asked Attar.

The voice replied, "It is not a question of anybody's sin – it is His absolute authority."

While Ghauth Ali Shah was narrating this strange story, all those present were aware that folded into each turn of the story were mysteries within mysteries. Then he recited a Persian couplet: "If he wishes for me separation, then I shall cry, and if he wishes me union, then I shall rejoice."

42

So Many Have Gone into that Fog

One day he said

All agree that the company of those who practise poverty plays an important role in one's transformation. These days, Ghauth Ali Shah pointed out, people enter into such company and expect that they can receive everything in a day or two, and there are those who are so deranged that they start examining the master–whether he is worthy of their obedience. First of all, why should one suspend one's own work and start working on somebody else's attainment? Even if we admit that a faqir may, out of compassion, attend to others' needs, it is unreasonable to expect that the dirt gathered over years can be cleared in a day. It is not in everyone's power to wipe out the wrong opinions accumulated over years and replace them with real gnosis. Those who have slept all their lives will wake up gradually, if they are really going to wake up.

Regarding those who complain that they could not get much in spite of their stay with some master for years, Ghauth Ali Shah gave the following story.

Once a guru was pestered by one of his disciples who had spent four years with him and felt he had received nothing, known nothing new, nor seen anything miraculous. The guru ignored him for a few days, consoled him for another day or two and then finally drugged him with a strong intoxicant.

After some time he asked the disciple, "What is your state now? Are you seeing something, some opening, some unveiling?"

"Guruji," the disciple replied, "I see nothing but a dense fog and I am lost in it."

Thereupon the guru said, "So many have gone into that fog, and they also saw nothing but that same awesome fog."

43

Imitating the Tiger

One day he said

Once a king asked his performing mime artists to simulate a tiger. They gave the excuse that they would prefer to perform at night because by daylight their skills might be exposed. However, the king insisted and further stresed that the replica should in no way differ from the original. The mime artists became increasingly concerned as to how best they could peform on a bright sunny day. One among them who was a drum beater said, "Don't worry, the date is fixed for tomorrow so we shall see how best we can manage."

The following morning the mime artists assembled in the royal court. There they consulted each other and the drum beater said, "Just cover me with a white sheet."

As soon as the white sheet was thrown over him he gave a cry of "*Il'l'Allah*" and emerged from beneath the sheet in the form of a wild rampaging tiger. It was as if a real tiger had appeared from out of the undergrowth.

The entire court trembled. The tiger paced to and fro moving from one person to another. When he came before the throne he espied the royal child sitting in his father's lap. The tiger raised his front paw and with one blow struck the child, whereupon, alas, the child died.

The minister in attendance said, "Don't panic, Sire. It appears that one among your mime artists is perfect. Command them now to bring a representation or facsimile of Jesus."

When the mimes heard this, the drum beater who had now resumed his original form commented that there was only one person able to mirror Jesus in this way, and that was Shams Tabriz. Having said this he disappeared.

Shams was brought to the royal court and people pleaded with him to assume the likeness of Jesus. Shams came before the child and said three times, "Rise by the command of God." But the child remained lifeless.

Finally in utter rage Shams stamped his foot and cried, "Rise by my command!" At this the child was moved to life.

44

The Man Sleeping in the Mosque

One day he said

Once a famous scholar and theologian went to the mosque for the early morning prayer. He noticed a man in the mosque who was lying on his right side with his face turned in the direction of prayer, apparently asleep. The theologian thought that the man had perhaps already offered his prayers and was simply resting. Later, however, when he returned for the midday prayer he saw the same man still asleep on his right side. Come the late afternoon prayer and again at evening prayer the man was still lying there. Just before the evening prayer was due to begin the theologian thought he should awaken the man.

When he did so, the latter rose, performed his ablutions and stood for prayer. Although it was evening the man began performing the "intention" for morning prayer and as he did so the day appeared to dawn and the sun rose in the sky. He then performed the intention for the midday prayer and it suddenly became noon. The same thing happened again when he performed the intention for the late afternoon prayer. Finally he performed the intention for the evening prayer and it was indeed evening.

After all this the man turned to the theologian and said, "You thought to wake me without recognizing my state. What is ordinary prayer worth in the face of this? For a faqir is always in a state of perpetual prayer."

45

The Faqir Asks for a Drink

One day he said

One day a faqir, given to drinking, came to see Shah Abdul Aziz and asked him to provide him with some alcoholic refreshment.

Shah Sahib gave him a rupee and said, "It is up to you what you do with it."

The faqir commented, "I have heard a great deal about your knowledge but it seems to me that you are still a prisoner."

Shah Abdul Aziz retorted, "Are you not also a prisoner?"

The faqir replied, "No, I am not."

Shah Abdul Aziz said, "If you are truthful in saying that you are not a prisoner of any path, then go from here, take a bath, enter the mosque and there perform *salat*. As you see, in so far as I am a prisoner of religious law so you too are a prisoner of your own thought. Therefore your freedom is only a fiction."

The faqir fell silent and bending down kissed the feet of Shah Abdul Aziz.

46

The Imam Falls in Love

One day he said

There was a nobleman in Shah Jehanpur whose wife was an exceptionally beautiful woman. Whenever she needed a letter written or read to her she summoned the iman from the mosque to perform the task. On these occasions, she always sat behind a curtain with the imam on the other side.

Once, it happened that, while the imam was waiting to pen a letter for her, the curtain was caught by a breeze and rose, fluttering, so the imam was exposed to her unbelievable beauty. At that moment, the imam was in the process of asking her what she wanted him to write but he so lost his senses that, when the woman started dictating, he found he was unable to remember how to write. Whatever the woman said, the imam could only mutter, "What shall I write?" As the situation continued unabated the woman realized that the imam had not withstood the impact of that fleeting sight of her beauty. She asked one of her servants to escort the imam back to the mosque. But his condition did not return to normal and he continuously repeated, "What shall I write?" Naturally people started gossiping.

Some time later the woman's husband, who had been away on a journey, returned. Hearing what had happened, he was distressed that the imam had lost his sanity. One day he said to his wife, "Prepare a feast, and adorn youself in your most exquisite dress and jewellery. I have invited the imam to join us for this feast."

When the imam arrived, the nobleman placed the dishes prepared in his honour before him. But the imam could remember only one thing, "What shall I write?" The nobleman gestured to his wife to come out of purdah and reveal herself before the imam. As soon as the imam and the nobleman's wife encountered one another, they fell into a passionate embrace and collapsed together. In that condition, locked in each other's arms they were buried. At the burial certain people tried to separate them but found it impossible. The nobleman intervened and said, "What God has joined together, let no man cast asunder." Neither love nor lover or beloved remained.

When God descended upon the mountain with His light it was rent asunder and torn into pieces and Moses fell unconscious [Q. 7.143].

47

The Washerwoman's Son

One day he said

Nizamuddin Aluya [d. 1325] was listening to the *Qawwali* and he entered a state in which he waved his handkerchief and said, "Alas! I was unable to equal the son of that washerwoman." At the time, nobody dared ask what he meant by such a remark. A few days later, Amir Khusro asked him to explain his statement and so Nizamuddin narrated this story.

Once, the son of the palace washerwoman fell in love with the princess without ever seeing her. The boy used to wash her clothes, fold them in the most beautiful way and then shed tears of love while adoring them. For a while he was able to hide his love, but a day came when his parents realized his secret passion and grew increasingly concerned. If the royal household came to hear of such a thing the boy would undoubtedly be sentenced to death and, even otherwise, so absorbed in love was he that he would surely pine away. The boy's parents were worried for they were poor washer-folk while the object of their son's affection was a royal princess. They were baffled that their son could even imagine a connection between himself and that girl.

The washerwoman began to reflect on how she might best cure her son's love-sickness and liberate him from its effects. So, one day she approached her son and sat down beside him in a state of utter distress and sorrow.

The boy asked her, "What is the matter? Are you all right?"

His mother replied, "What can I say, my son?" She started crying and then said, "The princess whose garments you used to wash with such loving care left this world three days ago."

The boy was deeply shocked and three times he asked, "Has she died then?" After his third time of asking he too collapsed and died. His mother started beating her breast. She had thought to cure her son by telling him of the princess's demise but in so doing lost him absolutely. She resigned herself to her fate and on the fourth day took the laundry, including the princess's garments, to the palace.

The princess looked at them and said, "Why do my clothes look different today? They do not seem to be washed or folded in the same way." The washerwoman started crying and this time her tears were truly genuine. The princess asked her why she was weeping so profusely and, in her grief, the washerwoman narrated the whole story. On hearing it, the princess promptly rose and asked the washerwoman to take her to her son's grave.

When the princess saw the grave of her lover she gazed at it with such intensity of feeling that the grave split open and she descended into it. A great uproar ensued and the king was informed of what had taken place. He ordered the grave to be opened and as he watched there appeared before him one body with two heads.

Thereupon Nizamuddin said, "O friends, such love is not the work of any shaikh or apostle."

48

The Nobleman of Lucknow

One day he said

There was a *nawab* [nobleman] of Lucknow who had a friend who was not only very dear to him but was also both loved and trusted by the nawab.

Once the nawab said to him, "You have been with me so long now that if you would like to take up some position or office, perhaps as a head of some government department, then go and meet the minister concerned as I have given him full authority over all such appointments. You know very well that if you simply stay here with me you will have all my love and friendship but there will be no material gain in it for you."

Thereupon, the man said, "I do not seek high office through your minister because I prefer to stay in your presence. Our nearness and company is far more precious to me than anything else."

The nobleman accepted this and said, "You must do as you think fit."

When the minister came to hear of this he was very annoyed and tried to send the man away from the nawab's court. When the nawab heard of this he summoned the minister and said to him quite clearly, "He is not under your authority. He is neither anxious nor intent upon gaining any position or job. He simply wishes to remain in my company. It is not for you to try and remove him.

Your authority is as one of the servants of the state but not over the servants of the king. So abolish any thoughts of hostility towards him that you may be harbouring in your heart."

[Gul Hasan says:] The wise may draw from this simple episode some very far-reaching conclusions; there is no need to refer to them in detail.

49

Laila Majnun

One day he said

When Majnun's love spread far and wide Laila decided to test how far his love was genuine so she sent a messenger to him and asked for a piece of flesh from his body.

Majnun replied, "Ask her which part of my body she desires."

To this Laila said, "He is not yet ripe and is still in the world of body and matter."

After a few days she again sent her messenger with the same request. On this occasion Majnun replied, "Cut away from me whatsoever you desire."

When Laila heard of this she said, "Now he is touching the frontier of love, now he is in the state of soul."

After some time she sent another messenger to enquire about the conditions in which Majnun now lived. The messenger returned and said, "He says repeatedly, 'I am Laila, I am Laila' in the same way as Mansur once said 'I am the truth, I am the truth'."

Thereupon she said, "He is now in the realm of annihilation in love."

Thereafter Majnun was found saying only, "Laila, Laila". This was the realm of *Lahut* [Divinity] which is that of *Tawhid* [Oneness] and later a state of forgetfulness descended upon him wherein neither Laila nor Majnun, neither self nor God, neither zikr, the act of remembrance nor one who remembers, nor what is remembered remained. Nothing remained and this is the state of Beyond-Being.

50

Sultan Mahumud and his Precious Cup

One day he said

Sultan Mahumud had a very precious cup. He gathered his entire court and placed that cup before them and asked if anyone could rise and break it into pieces. They protested, saying, "It is rare and precious – it is not proper to break it." Mahumud looked towards Ayaz, and Ayaz got up without hesitation and dashed it on the ground. The courtiers showed distress and blamed Ayaz for destroying such a precious thing.

The Qalander [Ghauth Ali Shah] commented: Nobody could know who obeys and who disobeys. Then he cited the Qur'anic verse: *He misguides and guides whomever He pleases* [Q. 14.4].

51

The Faqir and the Cap of Initiation

One day he said

To meet a great sage or a perfect guide is an everlasting treasure but such a meeting depends entirely upon one's fate, which is a strange matter in itself. If it is so destined, then it is the guide who reaches for the right disciple. So, as the story goes:

There was a man of God whose time upon this earth was reaching its end. He entered a village where he came across a boy, a weaver's son who was busy disentangling skeins of silk.

The faqir removed his cap and, placing it upon the head of the boy, said, "My Lord is calling me now. Look after my burial rites." He then lay down on the ground, and covered himself from head to foot with a white sheet.

After the burial rites had been concluded the boy separated himself from his people and sat in one place, silent and immersed in deep thought. His parents and other relatives surrounded him, crying and shouting, for it was as if the boy too had died.

Then the boy said, "Is it not strange that I neither went anywhere nor sought anything? I was unaware of the path that leads to God, yet God sent such treasure to me unasked. Now, I am no longer the same person. I am of no use to you, nor you to me. So leave me now and return to your usual business."

52

Insisting the Thief Be Initiated

One day he said

A seeker is a wayfarer. To seek is to rely upon one's destiny and if the seeker pursues his journey he will one day reach his goal. Sometimes a great blessing will come to the seeker from the Unseen and, although this is not the rule, most seekers expect to be blessed by such sudden guidance. However, it is only one among thousands who may be so fortunate. It is up to God alone to send down his mercy upon whomsoever He pleases. So, as the story goes:

There was a seeker who was looking for a perfect guide; one who was noble by birth, of attractive appearance, and whose knowledge and conduct were in agreement with each other. In other words, he was seeking for one who was perfect and praiseworthy in all aspects. Naturally, it was far from easy to find such a person and the seeker searched for a very long time without finding a single person who possessed all these qualities.

One day, exhausted and distressed, he decided that he would go out and whomever he met first he would make his guide. And there he came upon a professional thief. The seeker bowed before the thief, took his hand and insisted that the latter should accept his discipleship – that he was, in other words, ready to be initiated.

The thief was taken aback by this most unexpected request and pleaded with the seeker, "My brother, I am neither a guide nor a disciple of anyone. It would be better if you leave me now." However, the more the thief refused, the more insistent the seeker became.

As it was clearly impossible to get rid of the seeker, the thief, forced to assume the role of a spiritual guide, said to him, "So be it. If you are so determined, go and climb that mountain and there perform salat. When you reach your last prostration, do not raise your head until you are inspired with a guidance that will show you the path."

The seeker agreed, climbed the mountain and there he remained. God alone knows how long he remained in that state of prostration. Then Khizr [Elijah] appeared to him and asked him to lift his head, to which the poor fellow responded, "Who are you?"

"I am Khizr," came the reply, "and I have come to instruct you. The man whom you took for your guide was a professional thief."

To this the seeker said, "In that case I can't trust all this. It is you that should have come first. It is too strange, is it not, that I met the professional thief first and then, only through him, I was able to meet you. So, I refuse to listen to you."

Then, God asked Khizr to go and find the thief in order to instruct him first. Subsequently, when the thief had himself become a sage, he remembered the seeker he had met so long ago and wondered whether he was still in a state of prostration on the mountain.

When the thief discovered the seeker still waiting at the top of the mountain he embraced him with the knowledge he himself had received from Khizr. Thus both became the disciples of each other.

It is strange indeed that the guide received guidance because of the seeker and the seeker reached his goal because of the guide. "That was their destiny," said Ghauth Ali Shah Qalander, but one should not imitate any story one hears, for each has their own unique destiny.

53

The Soldier Serves an Old Man

One day he said

There was once an old man who lived on the roof of a house in Shah Jehanpur. He lived on the proceeds of magic amulets which he gave to people in need of help, and it was generally women who came to him for assistance. One of his neighbours, a retired army man, used to criticize him for his practice, claiming that he was not a real faqir but a clever hypocrite and unreliable as such.

After a time, the old man fell seriously ill. This gave the old soldier pause for thought and he said to himself, "I have constantly poured blame on this old man in spite of the fact that he has never at any time said a single word against my person. So, let me go to him and serve him during his illness so that he may forgive me for all I have said against him behind his back."

Thus resolved, he went to the old man, asked his forgiveness for not coming sooner and proceeded to nurse him until the day came when the old man lay at death's door. Sick and weak in his bed, the old man said to him, "Open that box." When this was done, the faqir took from the box one shirt, one loincloth and one cap which he passed to the old soldier saying, "These three things were given to me by my master and now I give them to you." Having said this, he breathed his last.

During and after the funeral rites, the old soldier remained immersed in sadness. On the third day of the rites, several people came to offer prayers for the dead man and after the *fatiha* certain people requested the old soldier to show them what it was the faqir had given him. The soldier agreed, but after seeing the garments the people asked him to put them on. He then rose, took a bath and donned the clothes. However, as he dressed himself in the clothes he became increasingly baffled. No one can know what he saw and what he felt. Suffice it to say that he left his family and home and took up residence on that same roof top where the old man had been wont to sit. There he took up and proceeded with that same work which had occupied the time of the old man.

54

The Jeweller Bequeaths Two Gems

One day he said

There was once a jeweller on his death bed who said to his son, "I am leaving a box to you which contains two stones: one a precious diamond, the other an ordinary stone. Both look exactly like each other. Therefore, you must take both stones to a gem expert so as to identify which is the real diamond."

So after his father's death, the boy approached a gem expert and asked him to identify the gems. The expert said, "If you enter my service for a period of five years I will tell you the difference between them at the end of that time."

The boy agreed and, during the five years he worked for the gem expert, many kinds of precious stones passed through his hands. Through this experience, he was able to attain the level of insight necessary to distinguish genuine stones from imitations.

At the end of five years the boy asked the gem expert to keep his promise and tell him which of the stones left by his father was really precious, whereupon the gem expert said, "The reason I have kept you in my service all these years is so that you could acquire the gnosis of the diamond yourself. Had I told you the day we first met, you would not perhaps have believed me or, even if you had, you might have sold the gem for a lower price than its real worth. Now, however, you are yourself an expert; you yourself have the true gnosis. What you do with the gem, I now leave up to you in the confidence that you cannot be deceived."

55

Initiation by a Prostitute

One day he said

During feudal times, there was a district commissioner of Lucknow who fell in love with a prostitute who was also a singing and dancing girl. Whatever he earned he gave to this girl and indeed he became so reckless that one day he was dismissed from his job.

One night he said to the girl, "Whatever I had I gave you. Now I am left with only this box. Whatever is in it is yours, but first sing and dance for me tonight."

The girl thought that the box might contain money or perhaps jewellery, and with this in mind she sang and danced throughout the night. In the morning she took the box back to her own house and the erstwhile district commissioner accompanied her. When she opened the box she discovered neither money nor jewellery. The box in fact contained a cap, a shirt, a loincloth and a coloured shawl.

The girl shouted in exasperation and anger, "What have you done? What sort of a joke is this?"

The man, who had lost everything, said, "Make me your disciple and with your own hands dress me in these garments."

"I take refuge in God," she said. "In your distress you have clearly lost your senses. If it is money you need now that you are without resources, then take from my house whatever you need."

"I need nothing in terms of money or material goods," he replied, "because what I had was all for you. All that remains for me to offer you is my life, so I place it in your hands. In the name of God make me your disciple."

She tried to dissuade him but so obsessed was he with the idea that in utter helplessness she called upon the assistance of her friends and neighbours and said to them, "This man has become really crazy. He refused to leave this place and I would like to get rid of him. Persuade him to take some money from me and then leave me in peace."

All this was to no avail. The man refused to listen to anyone. So the girl's neighbours said to her, "There is no harm to you in his request. If it will make him happy for you to dress him in those garments, why not comply with his request? Then perhaps he will leave you alone."

The girl finally agreed, took a bath and asked the man to do likewise. She then performed salat and raising her hands in prayer said, "O God, You are fully aware of my life and conduct. I am a sinner and as such not worthy of initiating anybody into Your path. Rather, I am being forced into this work." Having said this prayer, she placed the cap on the man's head and the shawl around his shoulders.

The ocean of mercy surged and overflowed. A strange sight then appeared, for, as the man turned to leave the girl's house, she followed him but it was as if she were being pulled by a force she knew not. The disciple was leading the guide.

They passed through village after village until they reached Gangoh where the anniversary of Hazrat Abdul Qudus Gangohi was in progress. Hundreds of people had assembled and the Qawwali was taking place. The man and the girl took their place in the circle. After some time, the man was seized by a strange state and he shouted "Il'Allah", and leaped into a nearby well. The assembly was frightened and some of them rushed to see if they could recover him, but the girl said: "What sort of Sufis are you? Why this panic and fear? If his state was true he will come out of the well, otherwise it is better he meets his death by drowning. Let the Qawwali continue."

As the music continued people saw the man rising above the well as if the water had swelled to the surface and he were standing upon it. One of those present who had spent almost all his life at the shrine wondered at the perfection of this stranger and, removing his own cap and shawl, threw them towards the shrine, saying, "Do not feel envy at what you have seen. It was that stranger's destiny and a unique one and, for that matter, a rare one also."

56

Kabir and the Burglar

One day he said

Once a burglar went about his business. The police on their rounds spotted him, grew suspicious and started after him in hot pursuit. To evade capture, the burglar rushed into the house of Kabir Das and panted, "I am a burglar and the police are on my tail."

Kabir Das replied, "Don't panic. My daughter is asleep over there. Go and lie down beside her."

When the police arrived at Kabir's house, Kabir invited them to step inside and search the premises. "You see," he said, "there is no one here except my daughter and my son-in-law."

The police were satisfied and soon left. The burglar rose from the bed and so profound was the impression made upon him by Kabir Das that he immediately became one of his disciples.

57

He was Asked to Go to a Prostitute

One day he said

Once an over-enthusiastic seeker went to a faqir to become his disciple. The faqir took out from his torn pocket a few coins and threw them at the disciple, saying, "Spend the night with a prostitute, then come back to me tomorrow and I shall make you a disciple."

That seeker was a very orthodox person. He said in his heart, "Let God's curse be on you. What a *pir* [saint] and what advice!"

Incidentally, the same night he slept with his wife and it was so destined that she conceived and eventually a girl was born. When the girl reached maturity, she started flirting with people and eventually ended up as a prostitute. The scandal made her father so ashamed before his community and he was in such distress that he returned to the same faqir and asked him what had happened.

Whereupon the faqir said, "Woe unto you. If you had taken that money from me and gone to a prostitute, then the entire situation would have been different. Now, as you sow, so you reap."

58

A Disciple's Dream

One day he said

There was a pir whose disciple had a very embarrassing sense of humour. One day the disciple turned up and said to his pir that he had had a dream the night before. The pir encouraged him to share the dream with him.

The disciple said, "I saw your hand immersed in a jar of honey while my hand was immersed in the latrine."

The pir hastened to interpret, "It is quite obvious you are immersed in the world whereas I am a faqir."

"But," the disciple said, "there is more to the dream." And the faqir asked him to continue.

The disciple said, "You were licking my hand and I was licking yours."

The pir was most embarrassed.

The Qalander commented: Such is the state of the pretenders of sainthood. The worldly-minded have five abodes in themselves: the washerman, the barber, the water-bearer, the latrine cleaner and the spiritual pretender.

59

Kabir Sends his Wife to the Grocer

One day he said

Once certain *sadhus* [Hindu monks] came to visit Kabir Das and he found he had nothing in his house to offer them as refreshment. In something of a panic, he asked his wife, "What shall we do? We have nothing in the house."

His wife said, "The grocer around the corner is an admirer of mine. With your permission, I will go and get something on credit from him."

Kabir replied, "Good idea. Go and seek him out."

Kabir's wife – incidentally, an exceptionally beautiful woman – went to the grocer's shop and told him that she needed certain groceries as unexpected guests had arrived.

The grocer said, "Of course, I shall let you have whatever you need on one condition: that you return here to me tonight." She promised that she would indeed return in the night after she had cooked and given refreshments to her visitors.

It was already late in the evening when Kabir suddenly reminded her of her promise and said, "Now go and put on your finest clothes and ornaments." Having himself helped her to get ready, he then said, "I will take you in the pony-trap as it is raining and muddy outside."

When the grocer opened the door to her, he was overjoyed, but was puzzled that her slippers were unspoiled despite the muddy conditions outside. Kabir's wife told him, "Kabir himself dropped me here."

As soon as the grocer heard this, his condition changed and he ran to ask Kabir's forgiveness. Kabir then duly instructed him in the language of his own trade.

60

The Majzub who was Fond of Kebabs

One day he said

During the reign of Raja Ranjit Singh there was a majzub who was very fond of kebabs prepared in yogurt. Once a man brought him some such kebabs which he ate and praised highly. As the majzub praised the kebabs, the heart of the man who had brought them became like a polished mirror and he was able to see sights from distant places reflected in his heart. He was so deeply affected that he took to wandering and after many months he eventually settled in Kashmir.

For twenty years he remained in this state of inner transformation until quite suddenly one day the light of that inner candle expired and he found himself returned to his former state. This threw him into a condition of such total distress that he started wandering again, trying all the while to discover what had really happened: how had he first entered into a state of inner transformation and why was it he subsequently lost it?

In the course of his wanderings he met Subhan Shah and asked him about this phenomenon. Subhan Shah said, "In my experience, such a thing has never occurred, either to me or indeed to anyone else. You had better go to Sulaiman Shah, another renowned Sufi, and ask him, as I believe he may be able to help you."

When the man approached Sulaiman Shah, he too expressed

helplessness concerning the man's predicament and said, "Our path is one of zikr and devotion; I have no clue as to what has happened to you."

Although the man decided to become a disciple of Sulaiman Shah, he never regained the state the majzub had conferred upon him, nor did he ever meet that majzub again.

I [Gul Hasan] asked Ghauth Ali Shah Qalander, "Why was it that the man lost his state after twenty years?"

Ghauth Ali Shah Qalander answered: "Whatever that man received he received without striving. Had he remained longer with that majzub, his state would have stabilized because the majzub was so perfect and complete that with one glance he could confer a state of inner transformation on another. In this instance, the man who received it believed he too had become perfect and therefore did not choose to remain in the service of the majzub any longer. Consequently his state did not last, for as soon as the lamp itself expires, there can be only darkness."

61

Bayazid's Open House

One day he said

Once Bayazid Bustami prepared an immense cauldron of food and announced that anyone who wished to come and eat was most welcome. Countless people arrived and all took as much as they wanted to eat. Both travellers and the inhabitants of that city came to Bayazid's door but the cauldron never became empty.

So the day passed and still there were hundreds of people at the door and still ample food remained in the cauldron. Then, a strange traveller arrived upon the scene. Bayazid's disciples approached him and invited him to partake of the feast, but he refused. The more they insisted, the more adamant he became in his refusal until Bayazid himself approached him and begged him to eat something.

At this point, he turned to Bayazid and said, "Agreed, but I eat only human flesh."

Bayazid, though baffled, regained his composure and said to the stranger, "You are most welcome to cut any piece from my body and start." The stranger replied, "Ah, and when did you become a human being? Look at yourself."

When Bayazid looked at himself, he saw himself in the form of a peacock.

Then the stranger said, "Give thanks to God that you have so far assumed the form of a peacock. When you actually assume the form of humanity, then you can make that claim. Are you not arrogant to call upon God's creation and invite them to such a universal feeding?"

He said this and disappeared. Bayazid wept at his words and asked his disciples to dismantle the cauldron immediately.

62

The Woman Hears a Faqir's Call in the Night

One day he said

There once lived in Delhi a beautiful young woman, the mistress of a certain nobleman. One summer at a very late hour of the night, she was awakened by a passer-by calling, "Is there any servant of God who would quench my thirst with some cool water?"

Rising from her bed, the woman picked up a fine pitcher full of cool water, and a clean glass. She descended the stairs and, standing at the door of her house, poured the water into the glass and gave it to the wandering faqir. He took the glass and drank it all except for a few drops at the bottom. Returning the glass to the woman, he said, "You drink those drops." Without hesitation she drank the remaining drops but in so doing found her condition changed. The faqir left while she sat down on her doorstep, apparently lost in another world.

After some time the nobleman awakened and, not finding her by his side, became anxious. Having searched the entire house he eventually found her sitting on the front doorstep.

He asked her, "What is the matter?"

She replied, "From this moment, we no longer have anything to do with each other. However, I ask you to grant me one favour. Give me a separate house beside the tomb outside the city so that I shall not go anywhere nor will anyone visit me."

It was agreed and she started living outside the city, beside the old tomb.

63

Luqman and his Son

One day he said

Luqman, a renowned sage, lent some money to someone. After a considerable time had passed, the man who had borrowed the money wrote to Luqman saying that he had been so busy he had not had time to return it. Furthermore, as he had been unable to find any reliable person to carry the money back to Luqman, he suggested that Luqman should send his son to collect it. Luqman agreed to this but before sending his son out on this journey he gave him three specific instructions.

"First," he said, "you will come across an immense tree at some point in your journey. On no account sleep under that tree.

"Second, you will pass through a big city. Do not stay there. After taking your meal there, stay outside of the city in the adjoining forest.

"Third, you should not stay in the house of the man who owes me the money."

But despite these very clear instructions, Luqman gave his son permission to follow the advice of any experienced traveller he might meet on the way even if that traveller's advice was contrary to his own three instructions.

After Luqman's son had covered some distance on his journey, he came across an old man who asked the boy where he was going.

The boy told him the story. The old man informed the boy that he was travelling to that same city, so they both continued on their journey together.

On their way, they came across an immense tree and the old man suggested they camp under it for the night. Luqman's son then told the old man that his father had specifically asked him not to rest there, but that if he should meet an experienced traveller who advised him differently he was permitted to obey the stranger's instructions.

The old man said, "Don't be afraid. I know about this journey. Just do as I tell you." So, both settled down to sleep under the tree. Late in the night, the old man noticed a huge snake slip down the tree. He killed the snake and covered it with his bowl.

At daybreak the boy and the old man continued their journey. The boy thought that his father had unnecessarily tried to prevent his from camping under the immense tree whose shade had proved so cool and comfortable. The old man read the boy's mind and so, to prevent him from disbelieving his father, he first told him about the snake and then showed it to him under his bowl. The boy seemed satisfied. The old man then asked the boy to cut off the head of the snake and keep it with him. The boy obeyed.

After a day or so they reached a big city. The old man said they should spend the night there and, though again it was against his father's instructions, the boy agreed to comply with the old man's wishes. They went to a tavern for the night.

Now there was a strange custom prevalent in that city: whenever a young man entered the city as a traveller, the king of that city would marry his daughter to the young man and the latter was always found dead the following morning.

When news of the arrival in the city of Luqman's son reached the king, the boy was summoned to the royal court where the ceremony was immediately performed to marry him to the king's daughter.

As the boy was on his way to spend the night with his bride the old man said, "Remember to take the head of the snake which you have with you. Before you sleep with your bride, burn the snake's head and ask her to inhale the smoke."

The boy acted accordingly. The truth was that the princess suffered from a deadly disease in her womb and any man who slept with her died instantly. However, the old man's prescription cured her of this condition and the boy was alive and well in the morning. This also brought the king great happiness.

The boy and the old man then left the city in peace. Eventually they reached the house of the man who owed Luqman money. The old man declared, "We should rest tonight in this man's house."

Although this was again contrary to his father's wishes the boy agreed. Now, this man who owed Luqman money was so wicked that he was determined to kill both the boy and the old man as they slept in order to keep the money. So he asked his guests, "Where would you like to sleep – outside or inside the house?"

The old man replied, "We shall sleep outside the house as the weather is hot."

So saying, they slept outside. Inside the house the two sons of the debtor lay sleeping. Some time after midnight, the old man awakened the boy and told him they should move inside as the air had turned chilly. So they entered the house where they roused the two sons of the debtor and asked them to exchange sleeping places with them. During the final quarter of the night the evil debtor emerged only to slaughter his own sons.

Having collected the money that was owing, the old man and the boy turned homewards. When they reached the place where they had first met, the old man said, "Farewell, my young friend. Give my greetings to your father." At this point, the boy asked the old man's name, to which he replied, "Ask your father."

When the boy finally reached home he asked his father about the mysterious old man he had encountered on his journey. His father told him that the old man was Khizr, the guide of the wanderers.

[Commentary by Gul Hasan:] The boy who went on the journey is a seeker on the path. The three stages are the three stations. The old man is the perfect guide. The snake is the soul. The king's daughter is the world as a mystery. The house of the debtor is the world as a trial. The debtor is the person imprisoned in the world. The two sons are the people of this world and the money is love or love of God.

Another meaning of the story is that whoever is perfect or a perfect sage will never prevent seekers of God from listening to another perfect guide. Indeed, the perfect sage might even insist that a seeker should enter the service of another like himself in order to benefit from him. Therefore the Qalander used to say that one should receive whatever is possible at the hands of a sage, irrespective of whether that sage be Muslim or Hindu, sober or ecstatic. Furthermore, one should receive that guidance in whatever mode it is offered whether by way of concentration, inspiration or instruction.

An apostleship may be concluded but sainthood is endless. It is possible that one saint who is greater than another may emerge at any time in this world. Therefore, one day he [Ghauth Ali Shah] said: "Muinuddin Chisti [d. 1236] used to send his disciples and followers to other Sufi masters of his times so that he could not only come to know himself through the eyes of others but also that he too could learn from them. It is sad that nowadays most Sufi masters disapprove of their disciples entering into instruction with another faqir."

64

Halting under a Tree

One day he said

My master Pir Azam Ali Shah once told me a story:

One afternoon we were passing through one of the districts of Delhi when we halted with our horse-carriage under a tree so that we could rest and then perform the afternoon prayers. A faqir happened to pass by and we shared our food with him.

Afterwards, the faqir lay down and we also closed our eyes. As soon as our eyes were closed we saw our carriage standing outside a large tavern. Some people were busy cooking food outside and to the side was the same faqir lying asleep. We asked the women who were cooking what kind of place it was and who owned the tavern. The women said that the tavern belonged to the sleeping faqir and that we were his guests. We remained there for eight days. Who knows what that town was, but it had no beginning and no end. The residents of the place were all cleanly attired, handsome and with excellent manners, and the bazaar was full of beautiful ornaments and artefacts. On Friday we went to pray in the mosque. Everyone seemed preoccupied with zikr.

On the eighth day, we awakened and found our carriage still standing under the tree and the faqir still sleeping. After the zohar prayers we continued on our journey. The faqir then rose and followed us. We asked the day, the date and the month of everyone we passed on our way and it was the same day, date and month on which we had started out. Naturally we wondered where those eight days had disappeared to.

At one stage in our journey we were obliged to sleep and stay in a house and the faqir asked us to bring him some bread after the evening prayers. He said we would be able to find him near the mosque. When we located him, he was flirting with a prostitute. Then, only a few minutes later, we saw him praying in the mosque.

As we settled down for the night, the faqir got up and insisted that we should take his clothes to the river and give them to a washerman. We were puzzled and asked how there could possibly be any washermen at the river at this time of night. However, the faqir was insistent that we should go there and do as he instructed.

So, we set off. As soon as we stepped outside the city, we entered a full bright day around about early afternoon, and there were plenty of washermen down by the river. We could not believe our eyes so we turned back by the city gate only to discover that there it was midnight and dark. So, helplessly, we returned to the riverside where one washerman said, "Give me his clothes." He washed the clothes, dried them in the sun, then returned them.

On our return we questioned this entire event. He said, "It is nothing but the invocation of the powers of imagination. It is nothing to do with faqiri."

When we reached Delhi we mentioned this affair to Shah Abdul Aziz, who commented, "That man was the Khizr of his times, whom we also call the Father of Time."

65

The Man who Said the Qalander was Empty

One day he said

One day a pious old man came to see me and after a while said, "I have heard much about you but you appear to be empty of any spiritual resources."

Thereupon I said, "Really, until now I did not know even that – whether I was empty or whether I was full. I have met so many faqirs and other pious people but nobody has ever pointed out to me what you have just said. All praise be to God that this knot was untied by you."

The visitor then left me and went to offer the fatiha prayer at the shrine of Bu Ali Shah Qalander. Soon afterwards he returned, crying and beating his breast, and threw himself at my feet, begging forgiveness for his earlier remarks.

"Listen," I said to him, "whatever you said before was your conjecture and whatever you are saying now is your thought. As far as I am concerned, I am exactly what I was when you met me. Your denial made me no less, nor did your affirmation make me more. However, you have not offended me in any sense so there is no need for pardon."

66

Junaid and the Wrestler

One day he said

Junaid was a superb wrestler, renowned for his prowess in this field. One day a stranger appeared at the caliph's court and said that he was prepared to challenge any wrestler in the kingdom.

The caliph said to this new contender, "You do not appear to me to be a man of any great strength. What makes you think that you are capable of fighting any wrestler in this kingdom? Indeed, the man I have in mind to meet you in a show of skill and strength is one of tremendous physical prowess."

Nevertheless, the stranger insisted, so eventually the caliph arranged a wrestling match between the newcomer and Junaid. As the two grappled, the newcomer whispered into the ear of Junaid, "I am a Sayyid and very poor. The rest is up to you."

Junaid fell in the first round and the entire audience, shocked and surprised, rose to their feet. The caliph refused to accept Junaid's defeat as valid and he asked him to go through at least another three rounds. However, in each round Junaid was defeated and eventually the caliph rewarded the newcomer, who then left.

The caliph was mystified and asked Junaid why he had been unable to wrestle successfully with such an apparently weak opponent and had thus allowed himself to be publicly humiliated.

The same night, Junaid saw the Prophet in a dream and the latter said to him, "Junaid, you treated one of our sons with such kind-ness that we shall treat you similarly." The next day Junaid resigned from the caliph's service and entered on the spiritual path. He finally became the disciple of Sari al-Saqti [d. 867] who was con-nected in his gnosis with M'aruf al-Kharkhi [d. 815] who was a dis-ciple of Imam Ali-Riza [d. 815].

67

How Alchemy was Taught

One day he said

There was a man who used to visit an old alchemist to learn the secrets of his art. One day the alchemist said, "Now, today, I shall reveal something to you of my knowledge." As his visitor was worldly-minded, he not unnaturally thought that the time had come for him to learn the secret of transforming base metal into gold.

The alchemist asked him to take a bath, put on fresh clothes and then follow him. As they walked out of the city and entered the forest that lay before them, the alchemist asked the man to sit down and wait for him. He then left, saying that he would soon return. One month passed. The poor man, certain that the alchemist would keep his promise, waited there patiently.

After a month, the alchemist returned and asked the man to stand up for a while after which he would impart to him the secret of alchemy. The alchemist then left the man, saying, "I will soon return." The poor man stood there for seven full days, and when the alchemist returned and told the man he could now sit down, the poor fellow was scarcely able to comply.

It was only then that the alchemist taught him the meaning of his art, thus freeing him from its literal connotation and, in so doing, perfected the man's quest.

68

The Hidden Hierarchy

One day he said

There is a hierarchy of the Friends of God [Aluya]. This is a hidden hierarchy, their grades and their numbers are known only to the One who presides over them. However, from sources which are reliable, we have received a certain description of this hierarchy which is offered here for the remembrance of the initiated and for the contemplation of the novice. There are nine levels or individuals:

1. The Axis of Guidance [*Qutb Irshad*]
2. The Axis of Stability [*Qutb Madar*]
3. The Homeless [*Qalander*]
4. The Hidden Guide [*Khizr* or Elijah of each age]
5. The Refuge [*Ghauth*]
6. The Changing Ones [*Abdal*]
7. The Fixed Ones [*Autad*]
8. The Father of Time [*Abul Waqt*]
9. The Child of Time [*Ibnul Waqt*]

The Qutb Irshad or Axis of Guidance [literally, axis of a grinding stone] is one through whom the creation receives both the manifest and the hidden benefits and graces.

Qutb Madar or the Axis of Stability is one who stays put because the axis should be motionless; who is by essence proficient; around whom the creation revolves. All relate to this one for assistance and support. Such a one is also called the Pole of Poles, *Qutbal Aqtab*.

The Qalander or Homeless is singular. Alone and individual, this one is carefree. The states of everyone are apparent to him. The traits of a gnostic are his own, without trace of imitation. The condition is that he should both be a mazjub, the absorbed one, and also an adept.

The Guide or Khizr is like the Khizr of scripture, possessing divine gnosis, knowing all mysteries. This one has the power to perfect anybody at a single glance. Only the most fortunate have the opportunity of coming face to face with such a one.

The Refuge or Ghauth responds to the appeals of the creation and deals with their affairs both manifestly and secretly in all justice and fairness. His sign is that he can dismember himself at will and regather himself.

The Changing Ones are a strange group, without whom the universe would be a perversity. They are seventy in number and can change their forms at will. No benefit accrues from them. They are assigned certain functions and nobody knows what those functions are. Whenever one of their number dies, they are replaced from the lower rank of Autad.

Autad is the plural of *Watad* which means a fixed rod of steel. Though we do not experience any manifest or hidden benefits from the Fixed Ones, their blessing envelops the whole of creation.

A Father of Time has perfect control over his states. He can create any state for himself whenever he wishes and can come back into awareness at will. There are hardly any people of this level in our times. If they exist they must be very rare.

The last in the hierarchy are the Sufis or Children of Time. They have a transparency between the manifest and the hidden, and are faithful to their time. They are obedient to any state which descends upon them; they cannot change that state at will as it comes and goes by the power of the unseen.

There are two types of majzub. The first kind is so through the primeval constitution and the second kind is so through acquisition ending in involuntary states.

The first kind is called primeval, because they are those who, when their souls first heard the divine question "Am I not your Lord?" and replied, "Indeed You are," were so overwhelmed by the vision of that beauty and majesty that eternal ecstasy descended upon them and they were purified of all that the lowest fringe of their souls contained. And when they descended from the celestial realm into the world of embodiment, their state remained uninterrupted, and therefore they wander through this world as if they are absent from it and they appear to us as insane and unconscious and they will pass through the middle world after the death of their body in the same state of ecstasy. They are content with what they have seen and received at the very first instant of their encounter with the Godhead. They are free from all unveilings whether of the world or of the self.

The second kind of majzub comes into the world fully aware and conscious like any other soul. Then he becomes a disciple of some shaikh or master, and goes through all the stages of instruction and initiation. When the moment of the initiation into the Ultimate Zikr comes, such a state descends upon him that he tears his garments, becomes unconscious and thus leaps out of the circle of sober gnosis.

69

To Hear the Voice of the Unseen

One day he said

There was a time in the past when Muslims used to take Qur'anic imperatives very seriously. Once, a certain Muslim heard the Qur'anic verse *Slay the polytheists or pagans wherever you find them* [Q. 9.5]. He promptly acted upon this imperative and invited the first pagan he encountered to a conclusive combat. They fought for some considerable time but neither one could completely overpower the other.

When the time for prayer approached, the Muslim said to the pagan, "If you will allow me some brief respite from this combat, I will perform my prayers."

His opponent agreed and after the Muslim had finished his prayers the combat recommenced. After some time the pagan requested that they lay down arms as it was now his prayer time. The Muslim agreed. After the pagan had placed his weapons to one side, closed his eyes and started his prayer the Muslim suddenly thought, "Now! This is the moment to do away with him."

As this thought came to him, he heard a voice from nowhere saying, "O unfaithful one, is this the meaning of Our word when We say, 'Keep your promises'? In this affair, it seems your pagan opponent is superior to you."

As soon as he heard this voice the Muslim fell upon his knees and started weeping. When the pagan had finished his devotions he turned towards the Muslim and found him in this state of great distress. The Muslim confided in him what the voice had said. The pagan was so deeply affected by this revelation that he was moved to accept Islam.

Alas! The Muslims of today are so egocentric that they do not hear the voice of the unseen.

70

Now You are a Faqir

One day he said

A cousin of mine was married at the age of seventeen. It was during this wedding that a faqir arrived and, as this family was hospitable to faqirs, he was given accommodation and he stayed there for nearly six months.

When the faqir seemed ready to take his leave, this cousin approached him and asked him whether he would take him into his discipleship. The faqir replied that he would do it provided his mother permitted him. The mother eventually gave permission, but added that he should not be made unconscious of the world.

The faqir retorted, "Once your permission is given, it is up to us what we do to him." The faqir called the young man, wrote a few lines on his forehead, and said, "Now you are a faqir."

I asked my cousin whether he felt any difference. He replied no. But that afternoon, while everybody in the house was resting or sleeping, we heard our cousin giving a loud cry. We all rushed to him, and asked what was the matter. He said, awestricken, that a red snake had bitten into or near his heart. Within no time, he was foaming at the mouth and his whole body developed sores; his eyes wide open, a condition of neither sleep nor waking came upon him, and in this condition he lived for a year or so during which, if somebody gave him anything to drink or eat, he ate and drank, but he otherwise lay in a corner of the house without saying or expressing anything.

Then one day, as if suddenly brought into a normal waking state, he shouted, "Brother, I am naked. Bring me some cloth, the faqir sahib is going to come."

As he said this, the faqir appeared in the doorway, and my cousin stood there with head bowed, wrapped in a sheet of cloth. The faqir asked us to fetch a cap, a shirt and a *lungi* [wrap-around worn by men]. They wore these clothes and went to a mosque nearby. Nobody was allowed to come in. The faqir then spent some time with my cousin and taught him a few things in secret. Then the faqir left. But my cousin spent the rest of his life in a corner of the mosque in a state of utter seclusion.

71

Ghauth Ali Shah and his Mother

One day he said

In my early childhood I was once annoyed with my mother. I was ten years old at the time, and I left the house and stayed some twenty miles away with an imam who knew my family. I didn't tell my family where I was going. They were worried and searched for me. After one month they located me in the village of that imam. Then my uncle was sent to bring me home.

The imam said, "There is no problem. This also is his house; he can stay and study with me if he wishes."

Then my mother sent another man of the village, now with a threat that if I did not come she would come and take me home, slapping me all the way back. When we heard of this threat we somehow recognized our fate and returned home. For a few months we were so frightened of her that we could not dare to go into her presence. Somehow we gathered courage, came before her and immediately fell upon her feet. At once, she forgot her anger, lifted me up, hugged me and showered me with a thousand kisses.

When the figurative love [i.e. love in this world] could overflow in this manner, how can we limit the infinite love of God which overflows towards this creation, because He loves us incomparably more than the love we receive from our parents? Our parents may look after us for some time and their love goes away with them, but He is always there to feed, to provide water, to bring about sleep, to make us rise in the morning, to nourish us and to entertain us by all the magic and jugglery with which this world is filled. There is no end to cheer and fun in this vast playground.

When Noah was distressed at the indifference and the stubborness of his community and cried, "O Lord! Do not leave any single disbelieving human to inhabit this earth," then His mercy, complying with His friend's prayer, assumed a marvellous and a mysterious form; He said to Noah, "Make an ark and welcome anyone whoever boards it."

But Noah's own son refused to enter the ark and instead he climbed a mountain and said that he was safe from the deluge. Then His voice was heard, "On this day there is no refuge but in Noah's ark."

And when a mighty wave was about to swallow the mountain including Noah's son, Noah complained, "You promised that you would not drown my kin."

The voice replied, "Noah, for your sake and for the sake of your friendship We drowned the entire creation, even though they were not excluded from Our obedience, for their mode of worship was not agreeable to you. We accepted your prayer and you did not care about those who were drowned whereas you show so much anxiety for your one son. Indeed, Our promise was true – he was not among your kin."

72

Abdul Haqq and the Faqir

One day he said

When Abdul Haqq Muhaddith Dalalwi came to the end of his
stay in Medina he saw the Prophet in a dream. The Prophet
told him, "Return to India and instruct the people there in hadith
so that they might benefit from you. At the same time keep in contact with faqirs of the country."

Abdul Haqq replied, "Apostle of God, how can I detach myself
from your threshold?"

To this, the Prophet said, "Wherever you sit in meditation in the
dead of the night you will be able to reach me."

The next day Abdul Haqq left for India and disembarked at the
port of Surat. He began at once to search for a faqir and at length
was directed to a street where one was located. When Abdul Haqq
arrived, the faqir was extremely excited and told Abdul Haqq that
he had been expecting him. Abdul Haqq sat down and the faqir
brought out a jar and a cup and offered Abdul Haqq a drink which
was prohibited. Abdul Haqq refused. Three times the faqir invited
him to drink and three times he refused.

Finally, Abdul Haqq said, "I do not object to your drinking what
you have offered me, but for me it is forbidden."

The faqir said, "You had better drink up lest you soon repent."

That night when Abdul Haqq sat in meditation, he saw in a

vision a tent in the desert and a voice said, "This is the tent of the Apostle of the two worlds." Then, a few metres ahead he saw the faqir standing with a long staff in his hand and however Abdul Haqq attempted to proceed towards the tent the faqir obstructed his progress.

The next morning Abdul Haqq approached the faqir and found him drinking. The faqir again insisted that Abdul Haqq join him in a cup but Abdul Haqq refused and said to the faqir, "It is forbidden to me and the command of God and his Prophet is preferable to your command."

The faqir reiterated what he had said the night before, "Drink up, lest soon you repent."

That night Abdul Haqq saw the same vision as the night before and once again the faqir was barring his way to the Prophet's tent.

The third morning Abdul Haqq returned to the faqir and the same pattern was repeated; the faqir insisted Abdul Haqq should drink and Abdul Haqq refused.

On the fourth night when Abdul Haqq discovered the faqir blocking his path to the Prophet's tent he was on the verge of striking the faqir but instead cried out in despair, "Apostle of God, I take refuge in you."

At that very moment the Prophet turned to one of his companions in the tent and said, "Abdul Haqq has been unable to reach me for the last three nights. Go outside and see who is calling me."

Both the faqir and Abdul Haqq were brought before the Prophet where Abdul Haqq narrated the events of the past three nights. The Prophet then turned to the faqir and said, "Depart, dog," at which point the vision left Abdul Haqq.

The next morning when Abdul Haqq went to see the faqir, he found the door to his room closed but a few of his followers and attendants were in the vicinity so he asked them, "Why has the faqir not come out of his house? It is already late in the day."

After some time one of the disciples opened the door to the faqir's room but discovered the room was empty. Abdul Haqq then asked them if any one of them had seen anything else leaving the faqir's room, to which they replied, "We saw a black dog."

Abdul Haqq said, "That was your faqir!" Abdul Haqq then narrated what had transpired in his vision and said, "It is now up to you whether or not you stay in the service of this faqir."

[Gul Hasan comments:] A faqir should not be so stubborn or insistent in any matter, for to insist is to display, and display is against faqiri.

73

About Tawhid

Tawhid also is *shirk*.[1] (The Qalander was discussing Tawhid and he was in a strange state as if the wave of gnosis was rising higher and higher.) Reality is above all oneness and unity, all knowledge and consciousness, so to call God "One" is also wrong, and now if you ask me why [the Prophet] told us, *Say He is God and He is One*, the reason was that as far as speech can go there was no better word than *Ahad* [Oneness]. So if we could leave every other thing and resign ourselves to One then this would be the most praiseworthy option. And if one is free from even that One then that experience is unspeakable. Let me tell you a story about this:

There was a Hindu sanyasi who was said to have been the disciple of twenty-four gurus himself. Among them was a woman. This is a story about that woman. When she married she came to her in-laws and very soon she started to participate in domestic work. Whenever she stood and pounded the grain she felt shy and embarrassed because she was wearing many bangles on both hands and those bangles made a lot of noise; she was worried she might attract the

---

[1] *Shirk* is the opposite of the Tawhid or Divine Unity. It is polytheism or any association of the relative with the absolute, even the idea of oneness with the transcendental One.

attention of those men in the house with whom she was not very familiar. So she broke one bangle after another and left only one bangle on each wrist. Then there was no noise. It was from that woman the sanyasi received his instruction in tawhid and made her his guru.

But the Qalander added, "She should have broken that bangle as well," for that one bangle was the trace of those bangles which were broken – Tawhid is renunciation of tawhid in tawhid.[2]

[2] Renunciation of the oneness in oneness; i.e. in experiencing Divine Unity you go beyond even the idea of oneness.

74

Ask What You Will

One day he said

There was an old shaikh who was always occupied with zikr and inner striving. One day he received the inspiration, "Ask what you will." He could not understand or make up his mind what to ask. He gave himself eight days to search for a sage so that he might ask his advice in the matter. So he went to a famous scholar and sage who was very well known and acclaimed and told him about his inspiration and the question that had been asked from the other side of the veil.

The scholar replied, "I am not worthy of entertaining this problem nor of giving you any advice on it. However, there is a man of God who lives in one of the city streets in the most wretched condition. Enter his presence, for he alone, I am sure, can answer your question."

After a few days the old shaikh located the faqir whose outward wretchedness was such that it prevented anyone knowing who he really was. When the faqir was approached with the old shaikh's question he said, "Very well. Come back tomorrow and I shall answer you."

So, according to the appointment, the old shaikh returned to the faqir and there he saw another sight. There was a huge uproar and there were lots of people around, and when he asked, they informed him, "Someone has killed an unknown beggar here. His body lies in one place and his head elsewhere on a heap of rubbish."

When the affair reached the judge he said in disgust, "Take it all away from me. He must be some vicious man. Pull him by the legs and throw his corpse outside the city so that wild animals may finish him off."

The old shaikh was shocked and perplexed by what he had seen and heard. At the same time he was also wondering why the faqir had made a false promise with him by asking him to return the next day. Surely if that faqir had been of an elevated station he would have kept his word. So, the old shaikh decided to address his concern to the severed head. So he asked: "What is all this? Your promise was to meet me today. Therefore you are under an obligation to answer me. If you are generous and genuine then you should be faithful to your promise."

Then he heard a voice issuing from the seemingly lifeless head, "O Shaikh, whatever you have seen now is the answer to your question. Throughout my life here, He was extremely kind to me and treated me with great love and affection, but during all that time I have never had enough to eat nor adequate clothing to cover my nakedness, and I have lived in wretchedness and poverty. That has been the state of my life. Now you have seen the state of my death. Without either shroud or grave, my head in one place and my body in another. Throughout my life I was unable to have a proper bath, to perform salat or to fast and now I am again deprived of the funeral bath and prayer for burial. And, if you ask me whether my faith and my afterlife remain intact I have no idea; no angel arrived at my death to ask for my accounts, nor was I given any news either of acceptance or rejection."

So, if someone asks for sainthood or aspires to become a *ghauth* [refuge] or a *qutb* [axis] let them ask for all these but never ask for love. So the eyes of the old shaikh were opened and he learned thereby that he should not ask for anything. For whatever He wishes, He will give.

75

Self-consciousness

One day he said

Once Ghauth-i Azam said, "When a believer in unity reaches a state of unity, neither he nor his tawhid remains; neither one nor many; neither self nor God, neither the worshipper nor the Lord; neither being nor non-being; neither Essence nor attributes; neither Gabriel nor the Qur'an; neither saint nor sainthood; neither attribute nor the attributed; neither name nor the named; neither first nor last; neither manifest nor hidden; neither paradise nor hell; neither light nor darkness; neither affirmation nor negation; neither heaven nor earth; neither goal nor station; neither the seeker nor the sought, nor the seeking; neither love nor the lover nor the beloved; neither Adam nor Satan; neither disbelief nor Islam; neither pagan nor Muslim; neither belief nor believer; neither the approved nor the forbidden; neither existence nor nothingness. Tawhid is through the renunciation of tawhid in tawhid."

The Qalander [Ghauth Ali Shah], commenting upon this speech of Ghauth-i Azam, said, "His speech is valid but he himself did not stay in that station. It is said that once a great light appeared before Ghauth-i Azam and from within that light a voice said, 'O Abdul Qadir, We have exempted you from prayer.'

"As he was a man of attainment he understood that this was an illusion created by Satan so he immediately took refuge in God and the light disappeared only to reappear in the form of a man who identified himself as Satan. This figure said, 'You did indeed save yourself for I have destroyed many of the high and mighty.'"

After narrating this, the Qalander said, "Had he not distinguished between beauty and majesty and agreed to what the voice had said he would have attained the state of Unity, but he remained self-conscious, and allowed his knowledge of distinctions to guide him, and also prevent him from advancing to the ultimate stage."

76

True Poverty

One day he said

Only one among millions may attain the state of [true] poverty whereby one gives up all possessions, both inner and outer. When it is so realized, it remains permanent and there is nothing that can abolish it.

Once, it so happened that a Sufi was standing on the balcony of his house when an uproar rose from the street below because somebody had fallen into a nearby well. The Sufi simply stretched out his hand from where he was and recovered the man.

A wandering faqir who was passing by at the time saw all this and, commenting upon the miracle, said, "My brother, all this is no more than child's play. If you really desire to learn anything, then learn [true] poverty."

The Sufi came down from his balcony, followed the faqir and asked him, "What is poverty?"

The faqir replied, "Poverty is that which is neither negated by doing what is forbidden nor corrupted by fornication. It is not polluted by drinking and can in no way be diminished."

Having heard this, the Sufi returned home and determined that, since the faqir claimed so much, he should be put to the test to see whether his words matched reality. So, he prepared a dish of rice and dog flesh pilau, adorned his slave-girl in a beautiful dress and, having given her a jar of intoxicating liquor, told her to go to the faqir and invite him to food, drink and sex.

The faqir knew immediately that this gesture on the part of the Sufi was intended as some sort of test. Nevertheless he ate the food to his satisfaction and then enjoyed both the drink and the slave-girl. He then told the girl to return to her master and inform him that such tests did not perturb him.

The girl returned to the Sufi and narrated what had happened. The Sufi was astonished and the following day he saddled his horse and set off to see the faqir. To reach the faqir it was necessary to cross a river but, as it was not too deep, he started to make his way across where he could see the faqir standing on the other side. In the middle of the river the horse both defecated and urinated. The faqir shouted from the river bank, "Why are you polluting the river?"

The Sufi replied, "Are you aware of the Islamic law that states that a flowing river is not polluted by urine? Don't you know even that simple law?"

The faqir simply laughed and said, "You are a strange jurist that you can on the one hand believe that an ordinary river is not polluted by urine yet on the other hand believe that the boundless ocean of divine gnosis can be corrupted by drink, sex and dog flesh."

At these words the Sufi was able to understand that miracles and obedience to law is one thing and poverty another. When the Sufi pleaded with the faqir to become his disciple and swore that he would abide by whatever discipline he imposed, the faqir refused and said, "Just give up whatever you have been doing so far. For until you renounce all the purposes of this world and the next, all degrees and all grades, all unveilings and all miracles, you cannot enter upon the path of [true] poverty. This is why there are so many who aspire to it but so few who attain it."

PART TWO

Discourses

1

Reflections on Divine Unity

Tawhid [Oneness of God] is an issue which none can decipher. However, there is not a single community upon the face of the earth wherein you would not find those who believe in the oneness and uniqueness of God. All the prophets and the saints and the guides, to whatever country they belonged, preached about this everlasting question. It is the pillar of Islam and the key to faith. It is the direction of all overt knowledge and it is the *K'aba* of every unveiling. It is the life of both the outer and inner paths; it is the anchor of all reality and gnosis; it is the pole of every obedience and the foundation of every wisdom. Both material and spiritual efforts begin and end with this. Its testimony is an open call, but its realization is a special invitation. It is so easy that everyone talks about it, but it is so difficult that the minds of even the elect are empty and scattered when they ponder over it. As the teaching of my lord and master [Ghauth Ali Shah] is solely based on Tawhid, I consider it necessary and proper to introduce the issues relating to Tawhid so that both wayfarers and seekers might draw joy and instruction from it.

The meaning of Tawhid rests on the judgment about a thing being one. Its knowledge is therefore its Tawhid. The Sufi sages have described and classified the knowledge of Tawhid according to their degrees of knowing and realization. Some say that Tawhid is of four kinds:

1. **The Tawhid of the Outer Path.** This is to believe that God is eternal by His essence, living by His life, listener by His hearing, seer by His sight, speaker by His speech. This is outer Tawhid, whether it is based on convention or on rational or traditional demonstration.

2. **The Tawhid of the Inner Path.** This is to affirm the unity of the sublime and the real by direct witnessing, through the light of faith, and to regard the addition of every other existence as nonexistent, or to regard the being of every existent as one in the Divine Essence. This witnessing has no need of any logical demonstration. This Tawhid of the inner path has three grades:

   2.1 *The Tawhid of Act.* That is, to regard all existence as the acts of God.

   2.2 *The Tawhid of Attributes.* That is, to regard the attributes of all existences as the attributes of God.

   2.3 *The Tawhid of Essence.* That is, to regard all existences as the existence of God. In other words, to regard the Absolute Essence as the only real efficacy and as the only real existent.

3. **The Tawhid of Reality.** This is negation of all otherness to the extent of the negation of one's own existence, and the annihilation of all the divisions of existence. Nothing remains except One Real Being and this is witnessed both in oneself and in every other existent. In this Tawhid there are nine grades:

   3.1 *The Grade of Intimacy or Interiority.* That is, that God with utmost nearness shines in the faith of the gnostic. *He is with you wherever you are* [Q. 57.4]. Self and intellect are annihilated in that light. It is in this grade that one shouts, "Glory be to me, my honour is great" and another says "I am the Truth."[1]

---

[1] The ecstatic utterance of Bayazid Bustami (d. 874) and Mansur-e Hallaj (d. 922).

146

3.2 *The Grade of Cosmic Tawhid.* As the Qur'anic verse says, *God is the light of the heavens and the earth* [Q. 25.34], and it is this that radiates in the vision of the gnostic so that he sees the existence of all existents as One. It is in this state that the gnostic utters the cry "He is all."

3.3 *The Grade of the Tawhid of the Name.* Through constant zikr the gnostic sees in the colour of each name the radiance of the Divine Essence. The power of zikr emanates from the gnostic and all otherness is abolished from him.

3.4 *The Grade of the Tawhid of the Attributes.* God radiates through the sense organs of the gnostic.

3.5 *The Grade of the Tawhid of Metaphor.* To the wayfarer, every single existent appears as truth itself, so that to prostrate before an idol is to prostrate before God. We see no other than God whether it is in the [Muslim] K'aba or in the [Hindu] temple.

3.6 *The Grade of the Tawhid of Act.* God radiates through the acts of the gnostic for whom the acts of all existents are the acts of God Himself. *He accomplishes whatever He wishes; He commands whatever He wills* [Q. 3.40]. In this grade both the victor and the victim are equal but the distinction between pleasure and pain remains.

3.7 *The Grade of the Tawhid of Perception/Witnessing.* God radiates through or upon the gnostic in such a manner that all veils of darkness are removed and a state of illumination follows. The gnostic is thus immersed in a gnosis without state, in a vision without interval. In this station the distinction between pain and pleasure does not remain.

3.8 *The Grade of the Tawhid of Being.* The being of the gnostic is annihilated in the divine light like the light of a lamp in face of sunlight, so that he becomes unaware of his own acts and movements, and in this state any differentiation between the seer and the seen is tantamount to *kufr* [disbelief].

3.9 *The Grade of the Tawhid of Total Abstraction/Annihilation.*
Everything is annihilated in the light issuing from the Divine
Source, so that nothing stays in the sight of the gnostic.
Through the lights that belong to the attributes of all existents he is freed; he is abstracted from the mixing of temporal and eternal. Then a mighty wave from the Ocean of
Beyond-Being overwhelms the innermost essence of the
gnostic and throws him away into nothingness. He is thus
immersed in an endless immersion and annihilated in annihilation. In this station there is neither being nor vision; neither name nor the named; neither ancienthood nor
nothingness; neither stool nor throne; neither effect nor
awareness – not even the knowledge of truth. In a word –
nothing remains. It is of this state that the hadith of the
Prophets say, "I have a time with God when there is neither
any nearest angel nor any prophet with Him." And then all
becomes One and it is then that we know the reality of
Whoever knows himself knows his Lord.

4. **The Tawhid of Gnosis [Realization].** When the gnostic has
passed through all the perfect stations and grades of journey
towards God, journey in God and journey with God, he reaches
this station of Unity which is the highest of the grades of
Tawhid. Here he is in utter nothingness and remains unaware
of self-awareness. This state is a reference to the gnostic's condition before taking on the compound form of the body when
he was one of the ideas, as is suggested in ancient knowledge,
or, as in the Qur'anic verse, *Does man know that there has been
a time upon him that he was a thing unstated?"* [Q. 76.1]. This
means that there was a time for man when he did not possess
a mental or theoretical existence, not to speak of an external
existence. It is said that whenever Umar Farouq heard this verse
he used to say, "Ah! Let that state be perfected again." That is,
to reach again that beginning from whence we started our journey, and to allow all and everything to be sunk in Unity.

In the opinion of some, Tawhid has its manifest, its hidden and its real levels or modes. The manifest level refers to Islam [surrender], the hidden to faith, and the real to piety and righteous conduct. Thus the reality of Islam rests on faith and the reality of faith rests on piety.

There is another opinion, which is a variation of a model described earlier, which categorizes Tawhid into three modes:

1. **The Tawhid of Acts.** This is to attribute to God all actions and objects of actions in spite of their multiplicity and contradictions.

2. **The Tawhid of Attributes.** This is the gnosis of heart which cannot be communicated in speech. Whoever thinks that the knowledge of this grade of Tawhid can be obtained through books is defective in his gnosis. Nobody has that knowledge, except those who are themselves perfectly realized.

3. **The Tawhid of Essence.** This can be realized only by those who have progressed from the Tawhid of acts and the Tawhid of attributes. Whoever would attempt the Tawhid of essence without going through the first two stages will go seriously astray. It is for this reason that the Prophet once said, "Give thought to the creation of God but refrain from reflecting on His Essence." To give thought to creation refers to the Tawhid of acts and of attributes and these two cannot be established but by virtue of Essence.

According to Imam Ghazali, Tawhid is the root of faith. The discourse of Tawhid is infinite. It is an endless ocean without beginning and without end. Its knowing requires the lifting of veils. One may refer to the four grades of Tawhid: one is the essence, the other essence of Essence, the third a cover over it, and the fourth a cover over the cover. Those who cannot advance without some analogy may refer to Tawhid as an apricot: it has one skin, hard and thick; another cover inside it, thin and soft; then the seed of the apricot; then the oil of the apricot.

There are some who say the testimony of Tawhid but their hearts are unconscious of what testimony entails. They are the hypocrites. Then there are those who believe from their hearts that their testimony is true. They are the ordinary believers. Then there are those who witness as they believe – this is the grade of proximity. One knows that things are many yet relates the multiplicity to the Unity that underlies it. The highest grade is that in which one sees in all things only One Existence. This is the station of the truthful ones. Here Tawhid is synonymous with annihilation.

There are also other opinions. According to some, Tawhid has four further levels:

1. **Tawhid of Faith.** Trusting the revelations and relying on the states of heart, one testifies in words that God is unique in attributes and worthy of adoration.
2. **Tawhid of Knowledge.** This is achieved through inner certitude which lends itself to firm knowing that God alone is the real existent and the absolute efficacy. The being, the attributes and the acts of all existents are immersed in the being, attributes and acts of God. Wherever one finds knowledge, power, will, hearing and sight, one regards them as reflections of the attributes of God.
3. **Tawhid of State.** While possessing the vision of the beauty of the One, the seeker has no awareness of Being until personal experience of Tawhid is regarded as an attribute of the One as well as one's own vision. Then only is the seeker joined with the unjoined and infinitely infinite.
4. **Tawhid of Divinity.** God, in His primacy, possesses the attributes of the oneness and individuality by his own Unity not by somebody else's. "God was and there is nothing with Him, and He is what He was" [Prophet's tradition], and He possesses these attributes eternally. *Everything perishes except His face* [Q. 55.26–7]. In other words, the being of all things is by itself lost in the Being of God. Such Tawhid is free of all loss, and

only this Tawhid is the truth.

Real Being is One. There is however one manifest existence, another hidden. The hidden is like the light which for all the worlds is of the nature of life. The reflection of that hidden light/life is the manifest existence which appears in the forms around us including our own form. The root of every name, attribute and act is that hidden reality, and it is the oneness of the many. All things in the cosmos are its lights. The reality of the waves is because of the reality of the ocean. Their plurality is relative, whereas its oneness is absolute. Sublime is He who creates the things and is free of them.

While creation is reasonable, the truth is a matter of feeling (or intuition).

This is the summary of the discourse on the unity of being. As far as the unity of perception is concerned, it rests on regarding all things as the shadow/reflection of the Absolute Being, a reflection reflected in nothingness. This shadow/reflection is not an individual self but only an image.

COMMENTS BY PEOPLE OF UNITY

The Sufi master Junaid said that the knowledge of the Divine Unity is separate from Divine Unity itself whose Essence transcends our knowledge. In trying to know that transcendence we move from our time to His eternity. Abu Bakr Wasiti, another Sufi master, says that in the Essence there is no trace of the creation, and in the creation there is no trace of the Essence (in the sense of being hidden). Exegesis of Divine Unity is one thing, and its truth another. Its interpretation is like the river of prophetic wisdom, whereas Divine Unity itself is like an all-encompassing ocean into which that river ultimately merges.

Understanding Divine Unity involves perceptions, cognitions, utterances and states, each of which demands affirmation. However, any form of understanding which affirms the Transcendent Unity involves otherness, and Divine Unity is pure oneness in which there can be no otherness. Faith steers its way through otherness. Faith is a mighty thing but it is not free from otherness.

Understanding of Divine Unity is like a lamp. Divine Unity is the sun itself. At sunrise the lamp's light disappears in the greater light of the sun. The light of the lamp continues to exist but now after a mode of nothingness. That understanding of Divine Unity which speech manifests is annulled by what the heart knows more, and what the heart knows is drowned in what the soul knows. Then whatever one says is from the Divine Source. Even then, speech as such is not Essence; it is an attribute of purity. Impurities of reason and heart have changed, giving way to purity – one attribute was replaced by another. When the heat of the sun reaches the sea and concentrates on it, the water becomes hot. The attribute changes, but not the water in its essence. Even the form changes, but the Essence which is formless remains unaltered.

It is impossible to apprehend the Transcendent Unity from the viewpoint of separation. It is a wilderness, vast and nameless, without sign or symbol or any observer.

Affirmation of Unity is therefore a falling away from Unity. Whoever testifies to that Unity remembering their self associates otherness with that Unity. Whoever talks about his own being within that Unity announces his fatal ignorance. Whoever sees his being along with the Being of that Unity is a disbeliever. Whoever seeks himself after having that [Unity] is an alien. Whoever sees himself does not see God. Whoever sees God does not see himself.

All thought and speculation are immersed in limitation and temporality. Divine Unity in its unveiling and witnessing is all purity in a station that is holy. Utterance and gesture, form and sight, idea and thought, life and feeling – all are the wrappings of the human mind. Recognition of that Unity is free from all forms of human judgment. The intuitions of the mystics are an image of that Unity, not its Essence.

Creation emerges out of the power of that Unity but disappears in the Essence of that Unity. If you deny yourself, you deny that creative power. If you establish yourself, you falsify that Unity. Neither affirmation is valid, nor negation. The One that raises before us a host of forms is the same One that annihilates them all. It is better to be annihilated in that Unity than to pretend to talk about it in terms of doctrines and stations of that transcendence. Abu Bakr Shibli, one of the early Sufi masters, once said that one who instructs about Divine Unity was an apostate from Unity. Whoever points towards It is a dualist. Whoever imagines It is an idol worshipper. Whoever talks about It at length is from among the unconscious. Whoever thinks of proximity in relation to Unity is far flung from it. Whoever thinks they have attained It finds their heart empty. Whoever is confident that they can reach It from within their self has lost it from the very beginning. Whoever seeks and gropes by their reason is all self-fabrication. Divine Unity is the veil of the beauty of Unity Itself.

Ibn Arabi [d. 1240] says that by abstraction we impose a measure upon Unity. If analogy involves you in duality, then refrain from it. If by abstraction you separate It, then you are a worse dualist than one who uses analogy. Some say Divine Unity is speechless because there is no addressee.

If Divine Unity is self, then truth is the speaker!

Divine Unity is the elimination of meanings from the Essence which stabilizes all divine decrees. Divine Unity is such that you disappear in It, and It disappears in you. It is ineffable Essence, not knowledge. You may have its vision without form but if you claim to know it, it is lost. Nobody "knows" Divine Unity except one who is alone. Divine Unity is the giving up of unity in Unity, it is forgetting through remembrance. The presence of Its Splendour is free of all associations. Divine Unity is both awe and wonder, a tremendous fascination.

Bayazid Bustami used to utter certain ecstatic words that transcended his self-consciousness. Once asked to explain them, he said that during such ecstasy he was some other being, not that Bayazid by which he knew himself ordinarily. Ecstasy is a loss of one's individuality that touches on divine self-identification. He used to say that after forty years of looking into his heart he knew at a glance that both lordship and servanthood are aspects of one and the same divinity.

Junaid said, in one of his ecstatic states, "There is no one inside my garment except God!" He also said, "A faqir is in need of neither himself nor God." In other words, he had gone beyond the duality of self and God.

Abu Bakr Wasiti said, "I am tired of that God who is pleased with my obedience and displeased at my disobedience as if he is none other than what I make of him by my acts."

Once when Shibli was discoursing on Divine Unity, Junaid was present and admonished him at his free speech. Shibli went into a state and replied, "I am the Speaker and I am the Hearer! Who is there besides me in the two worlds?"

When Shibli's end was near, his friends and disciples were all around him. One of them said it was now time to recite the testimony "There is no god but God." Thereupon Shibli replied, "When there is no other, whom should one negate?" As time passed, and as Shibli was about to breathe his last breath, someone recited the testimony aloud on his behalf. Shibli looked at him and remarked, "How is it that the dead give the last sacraments to the living?"

2

Discourse of Mahapursh Sanyas Mata

This discourse by a Hindu rishi forms part of the reflections on Tawhid. It appears that the discourse did take place in the fellowship as indicated by the inclusion of Ghauth Ali Shah's remark towards the end that Tawhid is dangerous for beginners on the path. It is not the actual speech of the rishi but a recollection by Gul Hasan.

All Hindu sages agree that there was nothing in the beginning except an undetermined state – that is, all Essence without limit, without name and without sign, above all sensibility and free. It is from this that earthly and celestial worlds came into being and all that we see here – the king and the sage and the crowd, souls and individuals, the Qur'an and the Gospel, the Vedas and Shastras, disciples and master, emperor and beggar, rich and poor – all came into being.

When all these disappear then that which was will remain and continue. Now you may ponder and, if you are true to what you know now, tell us then about whatever came, where it came from and, if it departed, then where did it go? It neither came from anywhere nor did it go anywhere. Being was not the "other" in the beginning, nor is now, nor ever shall be. "When I was nothing, I was God and, if I could be nothing, I would be God again. This 'being' has destroyed me. Had I not been, I would have been every-thing."[1] From the point of view of sacredness and devotion every-thing is a form, and from no point of view everything is formless. As a form in body it is mortal; as a form in souls it is eternal, nei-ther dead nor alive. So long as the embodied suffers from ignorance, it is called the individual soul. When knowledge dawns, its very reality is the Supreme Soul, that is, Being or God. When the body is gone, knowledge and ignorance as we know them here and all relationships based on our own feelings and thoughts also disap-pear, and also all concepts like "body and soul", "relation and rel-ativity" rise to a level where they are altered. Then what remains is that very Being which was before. And that Being is absolute motion which reaches everywhere. No! It is without motion, it nei-ther came from anywhere nor did it depart from anywhere to any-where. It has a place because it is in every place. It is placeless because no place can contain it. It is all-knowing because it knows the part and the whole of everything but it has no knowledge because it is Knowledge Itself – as there is nothing except it. What-ever names and signs we find here, that is, God and the Prophet, saints and angels, jinn and humanity, ghosts and devils, form and formless, heaven and hell – all these are myth and fiction and a product of the partial reason of humans. There is neither one who prostrates nor one for whom the prostration is intended, neither the worshipper nor the worshipped, neither Adam nor Satan. There is only One Eternal Being manifested in the multifarious attributes without beginning and without end. Nobody has ever seen or understood that. Above all understanding and comprehension, above all superstition and conjecture, such that was, and such that is and such that shall be. That neither decreases nor increases, nei-ther descends nor ascends. One and without example, unique and alone and one – but not even one because to regard that as sepa-

---

[1]From a couplet by the contemporary poet Ghalib. Gul Hasan inserts it as an illustration of the point in question.

rate from existence and to regard existence as away from that is sheer ignorance and stupidity. Who is the seeker and who is the sought? And what is the seeking? In this world people are busy in countless affairs and you can include among them God-seeking and God-knowing. This is an affair without top or tail. That pure Being is formless, without whereness and without appearance; Its attainment and Its reception an empty thought.

But humanity is attracted to many arts and skills. Whenever people concentrate on a particular art or skill they acquire an expertise and arrive at inventions which bewilder them. Such are those people who in their obedience and worship, asceticism and self-conquest achieve remarkable results and manifest in their lives great miracles and perfections. But all these are a play of their own powers because humans are a subtle substance – whatever we wish, we create.

For instance, when a sanyasi, through all his concentrations and meditations, perhaps even to the point of practising ritual or mystical death, reaches a point where he is now the centre of many miracles and unveilings – what difference will it make? What harm or benefit? What profit or loss is there for that Essence which is without form and without act? What did that sanyasi give to It? What did he not already possess that now It has got? It is what It always was. Its being is the same without difference or distinction in everything. But our sanyasi learned certain skills and undertook certain exercises and he was rewarded: initially, he used to see with his eyes, now he sees with his eyes closed; similarly he used to hear with his ears, now he hears with his ears sealed; in the beginning he used to walk with his feet but now he can fly wherever he wishes; now he can die and rise again; now he walks on water and still his feet are not wet – but all this is as a piece of juggling or magic. Whoever learns and has the ability to concentrate can reach perfection in all these matters. Thus, all eastern sages possessed these perfections but I wonder why these skills and perfections were considered synonymous with the knowledge of God.

Whatever is known is not God, and what is God cannot be known. And whether you have these perfections or not, what difference will it make? Nevertheless, where there is ability there is achievement, and what one has done others can do. That Formless One is not negated by negation nor affirmed by affirmation. It is not pleased by your obedience nor displeased by your sins. It is not happy with one who is occupied with It nor disgusted with one who is forgetful of It. It is neither near so-called gnostics nor far from those who are ignorant. It is neither the friend of the believers nor the enemy of the disbelievers. It has no relation with either India or Arabia. It is free from all association with either Hardawar or Mecca [Hindu and Muslim places of pilgrimage]. There are some who say "God ... God" and make their hearts happy, and there are some who say "Om ... Om" and similarly attain their peace. Some concentrate in their hearts and some bow before bricks and stone. All are Its names and all are Its works. Whether you give It a form or call It "formless", whether you say Essence or attributes, whether you call It guide or one who misguides, It is one and alone. Where is the other?

But Tawhid is an infinite wasteland and an awesome wilderness; only one among millions can make it their habitat. Therefore, according to the capabilities and receptivity of the common people, ritual and religion, Islamic and Hindu codes of law came into being as an instruction in morals, in obedience and worship, and to distinguish between good and evil. There is a community which makes idols and places them in the sanctuaries and worships them and thus finds its peace and comfort. There is another community which installs a mental idol and then bows and prostrates before it. For one there is a god of stone and metal and, for the other, there is a god in mind and thought. All this is again a product of a partial or fragmented reason.

All the avatars and prophets, all the guides and founders of communities and religions had an outward instruction suited to the reason and imagination of the masses and a hidden instruction for the elect. Whomever they found, at whatever level, they adopted a suitable means of instruction. Krishna gave to Arjuna the highest and hidden knowledge in the same way as the Arab Prophet gave to Ali and other companions a similarly hidden gnosis because they were the elevated souls. As was their knowledge, so was the knowledge they received. The masses could not have borne it had that knowledge come to them without being veiled in outward practice and belief. Whoever realized what they received, at the highest level, for them, every act and every mode became an act of devotion. There is neither good in one thing nor evil in the other. Hence, the elect also continued to follow the outward rules because they did not see any difference or any harm in them. They remained free from either expectation of reward or fear of punishment, from the greed of paradise and the horrors of hell. For them everything was right and in its place; neither does one begin nor the other end.

People say that the Supreme Soul, whether you call It God or not, descended at the dawn of creation, and this world was unfolded in that descent. First, knowledge was in the mind of God and now it is manifested in humanity; then it will ascend again and then the cosmos shall disappear. But things like this are spoken for the ordinary reason of the masses. You may ponder and realize: What has ascent or descent got to do with the Supreme Soul? Boundless and limitless, where is Its descent and where is Its ascent? First, God is regarded as One: One in His knowledge, and inside that knowledge is all this cosmos. When you say "God", then you say God's knowledge as well. God's knowledge is not other than God's Being. Thus, God's knowledge and whatever is inside that knowledge is All-God. Hence, there is neither descent nor ascent, neither increase nor decrease, and hence, when the cosmos was manifested – where was it manifested? Did it leave the divine knowledge and come out of It? No! Now also, all things that exist and all the worlds that remain continue to remain within the divine knowledge as they always have done. This is both hiddenness and manifestation. But, the wonder is that in the Being is knowledge and in the knowledge there is cosmos. In the being of humanity is knowledge and in this knowledge is the knowledge of God in all its infinity and splendour. One circumscribes the other. One is in the knowledge of the other. Which then is the circumference? Which then is the centre? Who is the Lord and who is the servant? But in our thinking here, in this sphere, there is no rest from duality and hence we distinguish and say "Lord *and* servant". The meaning of the Lord is servant and the meaning of servant is Lord. There is no anchor for this turmoil and no uniformity for this reversal. Whoever has known this and has reached this, for them all Vedanta and all Sufism is like the story of the partridge [see p. 66]. Only a few will understand what is being said here. The ignorant and the unconscious have no clue of the reality in which they are immersed. However, I neither am restless with them nor have any complaint against them. I salute them all.

This is what Sanyas Mahapursh said to the Qalander who in turn said that this kind of discourse was for the free and unlimited but was a deadly poison for those who are beginners on the path. Therefore, all seekers should either refrain from such a discourse or treat what it says with sincerity and steadfastness, always occupied with remembrance of God in devotion and in humility and awe. Nevertheless, this discourse is offered here as an example of the essence of the knowledge of the Hindu sages. It is an unsheathed sword and a cup full of poison for those who express daring without real gnosis.

3

Guidance through Hospitality and Compassion

Gul Hasan gives a detailed account regarding his master's daily routine and conduct during his stay at Panipat near Delhi. Some details are not only noteworthy for their spiritual significance but also shed light upon socio-religious life during the last quarter of the nineteenth century. Though great changes were taking place in the economic and political structure of the country, yet the eclectic ethos resting on the foundations of Bhakti and Sufi tolerance and mutual acceptance was still prevalent. Ghauth Ali Shah's personality embodied the best and the profoundest aspects of that ethos.

Though universalist and eclectic in outlook, Ghauth Ali Shah strictly observed certain basic values of Islamic spirituality. Apart from abiding by the prescribed rules of prayer and fasting, he would rise at two every morning and stay in prayer and meditation till daybreak. Soon after, there would be people at his door with all manner of needs and requests. He attended to each with respect and zeal, making one and all feel at home. Soon after the evening meal, he met with novices who required personal attention, and also met visitors and relaxed with friends. It was at such sessions that he told stories which opened the hearts and minds of those who were around him. These sessions would last till midnight in summer and till ten in winter. A brief rest for a couple of hours after everybody had gone was sufficient for him.

Ghauth Ali Shah did not instruct his disciples in any traditional modes of meditation, either Islamic or Vedantic. His instruction was internal and indirect through story and humour, through poetry and parable. His discourse was brief and yet there was a continuous unveiling of the mysteries while he spoke even casually and most of the time informally. At times, his speech was experienced as a wave rising from the fathomless deep. Whenever he spoke in this powerful state, not only our hearts but all the space of the hall where we held our discourses seemed to overflow with the livingness of a new being. On such nights, a gentle breeze blew from an unseen garden which had never tasted any autumn of this world.

In whosesoever company Ghauth Ali Shah sat, he appeared outstanding and dignified. His face reflected a strange freshness and youthfulness; the secret of that freshness seemed to be his manner of instruction, based as it was on symbol and parable. It seemed that direct speech would bring about strain and fatigue whereas symbolic discourse would always be refreshing. Whatever he manifested, from breadth of vision to profundity of knowledge and wisdom, he ascribed it all to God's grace and will.

Whatever gifts he received, he shared among his friends, disciples and guests. Unaffected by the status or possessions of those who visited him he showed respect and compassion to one and all. All his virtues both as a qalander and as a human being were reflected in his sense of hospitality. Whether young or old, rich or poor, mystical or orthodox, ruler or subject, disciple or stranger, all were welcome. He never sent those who were present outside the room when somebody wished to speak in confidence, but would get up himself and go outside to talk because it was against hospitality to trouble many for the sake of one or few.

He always preferred white dress and used to say that a faqir should not wear any other colour, indicating that as a faqir's self is colourless his outer garment should reflect that state. As a guide, he was a tower of magnanimity. Neither the devotion of a disciple nor its lack in some novice could shake his calmness and sense of detachment. Combined with compassion and hospitality, this inner detachment gave him a strange power but, more than power, it gave a restfulness of spirit.

Ghauth Ali Shah was initiated into all the major Sufi orders. He would bring to each one of them a fresh understanding when he spoke about them. He noticed a very close affinity between the Naqshbandiya and the Vedantic modes of meditation. Both involve an intricate structure of the human self consisting of a number of centres [lata'if], which are subtle localities of power, or lotuses of different numbers of petals in the Indian system. The system is generally comparable to the kabbalistic structure.

These are the six Lata'if in ascending order:

1. *Nafs*. Carnal Self. Location: below waist; colour: white, like moonlight
2. *Qalb*. Heart. Location: left of the chest; colour: yellow
3. *Ruh*. Spirit. Location: right of the chest; colour: red
4. *Sirr*. Secret. Location: in the centre of the chest; colour: white
5. *Khafi*. The Inner. Location: forehead; colour: black
6. *Akhfa*. The Innermost. Location: brain; colour: green

These six centres can be grouped into three pairs. The first two constitute the animal soul, the second two constitute the human soul and the last two constitute the Universal Soul.

The Divine Radiance descends to the first pair. Its self-consciousness is in the second pair and its embodiment is in the third. Ghauth Ali Shah described the Naqshbandiya method of instruction as follows.

The shaikh asks his disciple to sit before him and concentrate on his heart and hold in his mind the name of the Divine Essence, namely Allah, and then the shaikh transmits concentration and warmth from his heart. But this kind of focusing does not endure. As long as the disciple sits before the shaikh, the effect is there. But after the session is over, nothing remains. This first stage of meditation is analogous to a fountain of water. As long as the water is available from the source, the fountain overflows with water, otherwise it is dry.

Having acquainted the disciple with the first stage, that of concentrating on his heart, the shaikh leads him to concentrate on the right side of his chest which is the location of his spirit. When it is also activated then the attention is transmitted to the centre of the chest which is the location of the "secret" or the veil between the heart and the spirit. Then the attention is led below the waist which is the location of the carnal self and then to the inner centre, namely the forehead, and then finally to the innermost, located in the brain. At each centre, the disciple is instructed to hold in his consciousness nothing but the name of the Divine Essence. When all these six centres, one after the other and then all together, are filled by concentration on the Divine Name, then the entire being of the novice is overwhelmed by strange lights and states. If the initiate is sincere in intention and universal in outlook, he imbibes all those lights and then negates them under the negation of his testimony that there is no god but God. Then he moves ahead. However, if the novice is narrow-minded and self-centred then he is uprooted. If he does not lose his sanity he will not hold any light whatsoever.

But those who move forward experience both *jazb* [absorption] and ecstasy. Ecstasy in this context means that, when the heart of the novice is purified and settled, then the shaikh takes the soul of the novice along with his own, and ascends to realms that reveal such mysteries that the initiate is overwhelmed and experiences a state of drunkenness. In that state he is surrounded by such dazzling lights that he experiences total panic with no passage opening to take him out of that dazzling wilderness. He cries for help. Then the shaikh, through concentration, brings about the novice's relief so that he returns to his normal state of consciousness. Ghauth Ali Shah then refers to various methods which are used by the shaikhs to awaken the six centres of the human self.

1. To keep an eye on one's feet [that is, on one's conduct]
2. To be aware of one's breathing
3. To regard one's breathing with gentleness
4. To hold one's breathing
5. The zikr of negation and affirmation [*La Ilaha il'Allah*: "There is no god but God"]
6. The inner zikr of the Name of the Divine Essence [*Allah*]
7. The loud zikr of the Divine Name [*Allah*] twice, then thrice, then six times, each time striking at the heart.

There are other methods which are more general; for instance, some ask their disciples to concentrate on God as all-seeing and all-knowing so that their outer and inner purity is preserved. Others ask their initiates to concentrate upon God being near so that they can experience first awe and then comfort through the friendship of God. Some ask their initiates to imagine that they are inside a deep and vast ocean and they are drowned in it. This is called oceanic meditation. Others use the image of a vast desert for the same purpose, namely self-annihilation. And there are those who ask their initiates to imagine always that they are in the company of the Prophet so that they may have contentment and connection with his compassion. Meditation is a method which protects the initiate from chaotic and destabilizing thoughts, whereas unveiling is a process by which the veils of darkness are torn and entry into light is made possible.

Some of the shaikhs of our times, Ghauth Ali Shah once said, place an extraordinary emphasis on the need to concentrate on the face of the shaikh. For them the face of the shaikh is the middle ground between one's self and the higher self. This alone they regard as true poverty or attainment. Such exclusive emphasis on this kind of meditation leaves novices unaware of what reality is, what they are, from where they have come and what their origin is; and nor have they any clue about the Divine Essence and its transcendental mystery. However, a novice who is sincere may attain much even through this limited meditation. The highest the novice can reach is the vision of the ultimate middle ground, namely of the Prophet's face.

Once Ghauth Ali Shah said that the proficient was of three kinds – the perfect, the most perfect and one who is complete. The person of the first category is perfect in self and does not benefit anyone else, whereas the most perfect are not only perfect in themselves but also benefit others by both outer and inner guidance and intimation. But one who is "complete" may make another complete within an instant or within a year or more if it is so decreed by the Divine Will. The last-mentioned category is the highest in attainment and guidance. Unlike the traditional masters, this group of proficients communicate and transmit guidance and effects by their inner attention and concentration whether the seeker is before their eyes or a thousand miles away from them. They transmit their soul-aspect [i.e. their own middle ground between their lower and higher levels] into the heart of the other so that it becomes, as though incarnate in the other, like an imprint in a rock. None of the thoughts or actions of the novice can wipe out that effect. It remains permanent.

These proficients transmit their attention in three modes. The first mode is corrective. By this mode the master purifies the heart of the other, wipes the dust of remorse from it and uses his own will to adorn the inner life of the novice. The second mode of attention is intuitive. The master communicates with the novice intuitively, informing and enlightening the novice without physical or social contact. All communication of this type is on the middle ground of their souls, and it is a high level which very few reach and are worthy of maintaining. The third and the highest mode of attention is unitive; the novice is transformed instantly and receives all of the master's attainment without going through any preparatory stages. In this highest mode the middle ground of the novice's soul becomes a mirror for that of the master as though there is only one soul. Such an occurrence is rare. There are very few masters of such power and fewer novices who can receive the impact of such mighty attentions and survive to attain their own heights.

When seekers are stabilized in their meditations, then their guides instruct them in intellectual contemplation of the creation of the heavens and the earth, and of those signs which are around them and also in their souls. In such intellectuals, apart from the spirit of inquiry that is awakened, the novice may experience both immersion and intoxication with the world of meaning. The intoxication is an extreme sense of well-being from the immersion. When the seekers are confirmed in the intellectual contemplation, they are initiated into a gnosis in which all existents and their derivatives are considered as realities so that no mediation remains between the gnostic and the reality that is sought. Whatever one does and from whomsoever one receives hurt or comfort, one now regards everything as issuing forth from only one Existence. The seeker now takes the hint from the behaviour of the dog who does not run after the stone thrown at it but runs after one who has thrown it.

As in intellectual contemplation so also in gnosis there is both immersion and intoxication. Still, in gnosis the seeker as the knower remains apart from what is known, and is now led to the final stage, namely Divine Unity. As this stage is entered, what is known silences the seeker who now regards all accidents and existents as not only a manifestation of Real-Being but Real-Being Itself. The difference between attributes and Essence is lifted. If a lamp is lighted by another lamp, both are one light. There can be no difference in them. What is temporal puts on the garb of existence and assumes a form; it cannot be other than eternity at whose wish that form appears. Time and eternity are one fellowship by virtue of the unity of all being. There is no interval between them. The seeker knows God in His simplicity and singularity and because of this knowledge knows that there is no harm to his being; he is now one with all unity, whether he be slain or burnt.

Ghauth Ali Shah then pointed out that those who profess Divine Unity are of two kinds – those who are *hanifs*, that is, free individuals, and those who follow a tradition. The hanif is one who knows the Divine Unity without the mediation of revelation by another. Hence, obedience to a prophet or apostle is voluntary. The hanifs are found more among the wandering rishis and faqirs. Though they may confess their allegiance to one or other prophet, when they are in utter unity they are not aware to which tradition they belong. Those who know Divine Unity after a particular tradition abide by its rules and limits in all their conduct, both moral and spiritual. They believe in all the requirements of the testimony that God is one. Through their sincerity their hearts are overwhelmed by awareness of Unity, yet they remain sober and do not enter into the total freedom of an ecstatic state.

When the novice has passed through the four stages of allegiance – to the master, intellectual contemplation, gnosis of principles and derivatives, and knowledge of Divine Unity – he is led to the stage of freedom in which he is liberated from all lack and want. His "carelessness" includes indifference to whether he is sent to heaven or hell. Now he is happy, remains ever fresh and cheerful. He now looks at both the rich and the poor around him without agitation.

When the novice has covered these five stages, he is then brought to the point where he experiences annihilation. He is taught that everything he sees from the heavens to the earth, all existents including himself, are all extinct except one ever-living Reality, one absolute transcendent Essence. At this stage the seeker is drowned in what he knows not, a state neither of consciousness nor of unconsciousness. When all these six stages are completed, the novice is an adept. He is ready to leave the stage of annihilation and enter into the stage of everlastingness. From this stage, union is only one step away. Here neither any master's attention nor any adept's effort avails. Nobody can take anybody else for the final embrace. There one goes alone – alone to alone.

All these seven stages are branches, each branch culminating in a different fruit: remembrance leads to yearning; intellection leads to love; immersion and intoxication to gnosis; wakefulness to Divine Unity; happiness to freedom; absorption to annihilation; and regathering of self leads to everlastingness.

Once Ghauth Ali Shah was asked about unveiling. Thereupon he said that unveiling is of two kinds – one of the cosmos and another of the self. In the first unveiling the cosmos reveals its secrets gradually in accord with the seeker's levels of development. The unveiling of the self is in reality a reference to the Divine Essence. As soon as one concentrates on the Divine Essence, there is a flood of lights and darknesses. This is the realm of attributes. The traveller should move ahead and concentrate on pure simplicity, on oneness without any attribution. One now goes through emptiness and fullness of being. A state of bewilderment descends. Only a few stand firm and reach their ultimate goal. Others, those who are sincere, remain perpetually restless as they are unable to rise above their sense of wonder. Let one who aspires to such heights seek a person of God and surrender to his guidance and gnosis so that one day the image is absorbed in the original. If one stays in the certitude of knowledge, one is far away from one's goal. If one goes to the certitude of vision, then one is near. But the one who reaches the certitude of essence has already arrived.

Ghauth Ali Shah was also asked about the majzubs. They are of two kinds, he said, and they are primary and secondary.[1] The primary ones are those whose souls, when they heard the Divine Call [at creation] *Am I not your Lord?* [Q. 7.172], were so overwhelmed by what they saw of the glory and majesty of their Lord that they were cleansed of all yearnings for anything from both the worlds, and when they left the intelligible world and entered this world they remained unaware of the place to which they had come. Their ecstasy remains without interval, and in the same state they go away from this world and pass through all the worlds. Their knowledge is what they received at the dawn of creation. Unveilings of cosmos

---

[1] A reference to the two types of majzub (those absorbed in apparently insane states) is made in "The Hidden Hierarchy", story 68. Here Gul Hasan repeats the same in different words and elaborates.

or of self are not for them. They neither guide nor misguide anyone.

The second type of majzub enters the world awake and behaves reasonably for a long time but at one glance from a proficient is so overwhelmed that he loses his sanity and enters the state of bewilderment and self-destruction. At times he goes through unveilings of mysteries, and whatever he learns and sees he reveals either by enigmatic utterances or when fully awake, however briefly, by intelligent and understandable discourse. These majzubs are mostly drawn to the unveiling of the world of attributes. Both kinds of majzub are a phenomenon and a sign. A majzub does not guide or benefit anyone except that he might turn somebody into his own likeness. The station of seeker is therefore greater than that of majzub.

Then Ghauth Ali Shah gave a clear warning that seekers who enter one mystical order or another should strictly follow the rules of that order. If they are initiated into more than one order, they should not follow rules that contradict one another but adhere to one set of rules at one time. For instance, the Qadriya and the Chishtiya orders allow loud chanting which, within their meditative provisions, leads to the opening of the heart and tasting of celestial happiness, whereas the Naqshbandiya and the Suhrawardiya orders do not encourage it. Each tree of gnosis in a given soil requires a different type of nurturing and watering.

One night while discussing how, in esoteric poetry of all cultures and religions, powerful techniques of meditation are concealed under ordinary metaphors, Ghauth Ali Shah gave us specific examples. When wine is mentioned, it represents love; when reference is made to the scripture, it means humanity; when K'aba is mentioned, it is a symbol of the heart; and when temple is suggested, it is a reference to the vision of the master's face during meditation. In Persian poetry, when we are asked not to hurt humanity, it means that we should keep our eyelashes still, and keep our eyes closed and steadfast during meditation. Similarly in Kabir Das, Ghauth Ali Shah said, we come across references to such techniques as equalizing the breath through both the nostrils so that the heart's rhythm is balanced and serves as a base on which to elevate consciousness.[2] The ascending consciousness is also the objective of another practice by which all the three eyes [the two physical eyes and the inner eye] are brought to one point of concentration in the mind in which one may expect a tremendous explosion. If the novice has dared to practise this alone, then he will collapse and lose his sanity. But if he is under the guidance of a proficient, then his whole being will be filled with light.

When someone raised the question of the variety of paths and techniques linked with several doctrines, Ghauth Ali Shah set them all aside by a gesture of his hand. Of course, he said, there are some who believe that God alone is all-powerful and humanity has no free will. Some say that both God and humanity have free will but humanity is subservient to God. There are those who regard goodness as originating from God whereas they attribute evil, if any, to themselves. Likewise regarding attainment, they have various doctrines.

On the subject of Divine Unity, some discourse about the unity of All-Being; others aspire to its vision; some strive for union; and there are those who are incarnationists. Some are satisfied with the image of unity in their souls, and others go for Essence. Some say, "That is" and do not say more. "All is from that" or "All is that"; such is the variety of insights.

So let them all strive, he said, in their own ways towards that mystery – the traditionalists with their obedience to the law and ritual, and mystics with their meditations and aspirations, and the madmen with their eyes filled with wonder. *We are of God, and unto God we all return* [Q. 2.156].

When asked about those who are on the right path and those who go astray, he cited the Qur'anic utterance that all things that

---

[2] Kabir Das was a fifteenth-century mystic, poet and religious reformer born into a family of weavers in Benares.

move are held by God and God is on the straight path [Q. 11.56]. Asked about how the truth of the Divine Reality is manifested in creation, he cited Junaid when he said, "Look around! It is the truth."

Once Ghauth Ali Shah said that there are two kinds of people who practise poverty: those who strive, and those who are resigned to the divine decree. Then he smiled and said that even those who make an effort are pulled by divine attraction. However, he added, both of them should know that they already possess within themselves what they strive for, or rest upon. When asked how far the perfect ones go, he replied that they all go up to the divine threshold, the stage of the ultimate attainment of their selfhood, and beyond that nobody knows.

PART THREE

Life and Times of Ghauth Ali Shah

1

Family and Spiritual Genealogy

Ghauth Ali Shah's ancestors came from Kurasan [Iran] into India, first settling in Multan and later in Sind. Ghauth Ali Shah's grandfather, Sayyid Zahur al-Hassan, a very pious and respected person, made Bihar [north-east India] his home. Ghauth Ali Shah was born on Friday 7 December 1804. As his mother was not well and was advised not to feed him, a wet nurse was soon found in the neighbourhood. She was the wife of Pandit Ram Sanihi, a pious and God-fearing man.

Each one of them gave him a different name. His grandfather called him "Kurshid Ali" [One who shines in the Light of Ali], his father addressed him as "Abul Hasan" [Father of Hasan, one of the titles of Ali] while his mother named him "Ghauth Ali" [One who is under the protection of Ali]. His wet nurse looked upon him as "Ganga Bishan" [One who is an offering to the Ganges].

It was at the start of his fourth year that his mother began to teach him to recite and read the Qur'an, and Pandit Ram Sanihi, whose wife was his wet nurse, taught him Sanskrit and made him familiar with the Hindu scriptures. His father's other wife taught him Persian, while her father gave him the first lessons in Arabic grammar. Ghauth Ali Shah recalls all his teachers with love and gratitude, particularly the wife of one of his teachers, Fazl-e Imam

Khairabadi. She treated him with such love and generosity that soon after her death Ghauth Ali Shah gave up learning from books as if she had revealed to him that real knowledge resides only in a loving heart. Whatever he had learnt during the first twelve years of his life was to be deepened and enriched in time to come, when he left his home to become homeless, to come home to truth.

Ghauth Ali Shah was a nomad at heart, his soul, like that of Hagar, going through the wilderness of this world in search of "water", the true gnosis which alone can quench the soul's thirst. This yearning for self-knowledge was an integral part of his constitution whose heredity goes back through thirty-two generations to the Prophet. Ghauth Ali Shah was a *sayyid*, one who had descended from the Prophet's family, through his daughter, Fatima.

Genealogy from the Qalander to the Prophet
Ghauth Ali Shah
Ahmad Hasan
Zahur al-Hasan
Mohammed Ali
Hamid Hasan
Hamid Ali
Abu Sayeed
Muslehuddin
Mubarak
Haqqani
Mohammed Ghauth Shamsuddin
Sah Sayyid Amir
Abul Hasan
Abu Ali
Mas'ood Nurruddin
Abul Abbas Ahmad
Safiuddin
Abdul Wahhab
Abdul Qadir Jilani

Abu Saleh
Musa Salith
Abdullah Salith
Mohammed Zahid
Mohammed Rumi
Sayyid Da'ud
Sayyid Musa Thani
Sayyid Abdullah Thani
Sayyid Musa
Sayyid Mohsin Abdallah
Hasan Muthanna
Imam Hasan
Fatima Zahra
Mohammed Mustafa (The Apostle of God)

In accord with the tradition of the Family of the Prophet, Ghauth Ali Shah first took his own father as his spiritual guide, a son changing into a disciple. Then his father, seeing that his son's thirst for knowledge was vast, took him wherever he could and brought him into the company of other masters from various mystical orders.

Ghauth Ali Shah was initiated at a very early age into three major Sufi orders: Suhrawardiya [assuming a distinct identity in the thirteenth century], Qadriya and Naqshbandiya [originating in the twelfth and fourteenth centuries respectively].

Ghauth Ali Shah was initiated into several dimensions of mystical life by nineteen spiritual elders, eleven of whom were Muslim and eight of whom were Hindu.[1]

---

[1] We therefore have in Ghauth Ali Shah's life the richest and rarest convergence of the two mighty streams of spirituality, the Islamic and the Vedantic.

2

Early Experiences and Subsequent Travels

One of the events in his early life which had a deep impact on Ghauth Ali Shah related to his mysterious uncle who earned his livelihood by entertaining people during festivals and family ceremonies. The uncle engaged in the ancient profession of enacting unpredictable combinations of idiotic and spiritually inspired states, say, as depicted by the character of the Fool. However much the elders of the family tried to dissuade him from this profession, he persisted and, to silence them, said that Abdul Qadir Jilani [d. 1166], the founder of the Qadriya spiritual order, had commanded him through a dream to practise that art.

Once, playing several roles to entertain a marriage party, he entered into one of his mysterious states, a state beside himself. Amidst that fun and merriment while he was being laughed at and mocked, he remained calm. However, the bridegroom, who was leading the laughter of the crowd, started to imitate him particularly while he was playing a female role. He tolerated this for some time and then, in a voice which was linked with his inner state, he turned towards the bridegroom and said, "Why, why are you behaving like a woman?" As soon as the word was uttered, the bridegroom became, to all appearances, a woman. The marriage party was cancelled. The bridegroom's family encircled this mysterious clown whose one word had the power to transform one thing into another. Asked to explain how it happened, he said, "In those moments it is not my tongue which speaks, nor have I any power over it." Then he added, "Let us have another party and let people assemble again, and if he mocks me again, let us see what word issues forth."

So the party was reassembled. The entertainer started his act. It appeared as if everything was happening for the first time, such was the spontaneity of the clown. At the moment when the bridegroom started to tease the actor and went beyond the limits of decency, he looked at him and said with an unusual voice of authority, "Lad! restrain yourself!" As soon as the word was heard, the addressee followed it by assuming that form, returning to his original identity. *Truly, when He intends a thing, His command is, "Be", and it is* [Q. 36.82].

After this incident he was no longer seen at any festival or ceremony, and it was said that he was living in a far-off village by the Ganges. Once the village was threatened by the rising waters of the river. His neighbours asked him to join them in raising a temporary dam to prevent the waters from engulfing the village. He did join them but, instead of helping them raise the dam, he started cutting the ground in favour of the expanding river. The people of the village were infuriated and considered him as some madman who did not know what he was doing. But after a while they noticed that the river was withdrawing and actually changing its course. They were perplexed and asked him about the meaning of his irrational act. He replied, "I just co-operated with the river and with One who has power over the river and, when we acted according to His will, he showed compassion and we were saved from the oncoming flood."

During his childhood Ghauth Ali Shah came to know of several such stories, one more unbelievable than the other – stories relating to strange powers. There were people, he was told, who go through physical barriers as if they were subtle substance. He met a *babaji*

179

[a term of affection for a sage] in Dehra Dun who could recreate himself every seventy years. He knew about his own cousin who not only saw visions of strange worlds but also made others see them by closing their eyes with his hands. Once he transported his father and mother into another world for seven days, and when they opened their eyes they had closed their eyes upon this world for only a couple of seconds. Ghauth Ali Shah was told that this cousin of his was not an ordinary human being but belonged to the hidden hierarchy of noble beings who were called *abdal*, "those who change their forms and locations by free will alone".

Ghauth Ali Shah told of an encounter under extraordinary circumstances with a majzub with the strange name of Kafir Shah [the King of the Disbelievers]. One evening by a lake far away from any village he found him dying of some strange sickness. Some time after Ghauth Ali Shah's arrival in his presence, the majzub's condition deteriorated. He closed his eyes for a while and then, while covering his face, said, "Salaam 'alaikum", and passed away. Ghauth Ali Shah decided to stay by the body till morning and then seek help to bury him. After a couple of hours he thought of performing his final prayers for the night. He had to go to the lake to perform his ritual washing of hands, face and feet but he was hesitant to leave the body exposed to the abuse of any wild animal of the jungle. While he hesitated, in two minds whether to leave the body or stay, to his total shock, the majzub sat up and said in a loud clear voice, "Il'l'Allah". Being young and still inexperienced about such mysteries, Ghauth Ali Shah thought that a wandering ghost had entered into the majzub's body.

To remove any such superstititon, the "risen" majzub said, "Don't be frightened, I am the same Kafir Shah – I have taken leave from the other side until mid-day tomorrow, so go now and offer your prayers."

After prayers Ghauth Ali Shah asked him who he really was, how he could attain such powers, and into what world he entered after his death. He replied, "I am a prince of the Taimuri family and this power I received by my communion with another elevated soul, and, as regards what I saw on the other side, it is so vastly different from what you can imagine that it is better that you see it yourself when you cross the final frontier."

The following day at the appointed time he had mentioned, he said farewell. He told Ghauth Ali Shah not to worry about his burial as another qalander was on his way to bury him. Then he lay down and after pointing first to his feet and then to his waist to show his body was dying, he finally pointed to his throat and, before closing his eyes said "Salaam 'alaikum."

Ghauth Ali Shah also saw those pirs who had a crowd of disciples over whom they presided without any compassion whatsoever. Ghauth Ali Shah would approach them and warn them to fear God who alone was worthy of total submission and who alone had the freedom to lay any burdens upon them.

Though well acquainted with several techniques and levels of meditation and while aware of the aspirations of both the novice and the adept for the visions of the higher order, Ghauth Ali Shah found all of it empty of God, all nothing but the magic of one's heightened attention and excited imagination. Once asked why he hesitated to say "All is that", he replied, "Those who say it are empty of it, and those who are filled with it do not say it."

Once Ghauth Ali Shah visited a [Hindu] temple in the early hours of the morning. A young pandit was concluding his discourse on Divine Unity. The worship soon commenced accompanied by the music in the mode of the hour. The effect of that music at that hour lasted in his soul, as Ghauth Ali Shah remarked, for several days. However, he remained critical of ecstasy that was brought about by external means, even one as great as music. He always valued the inner resources within one's own self, namely purity of intention, sincerity in devotion and loneliness in prayer.

Though critical of the prevalent preoccupation with the mystical states and with the powers of concentration, Ghauth Ali Shah admitted the presence of certain exceptional people who are beings of a totally different order. The following episode bears this out.

Once, outside a village, Ghauth Ali Shah came across a boy of thirteen or fourteen sitting in *samadhi* [meditation], his eyes open and yet seemingly sightless as though focused on formlessness. As we were watching the boy, Ghauth Ali Shah said, his father came out of his house and stood beside us, and when we looked to him, mystified by the deep presence which the boy emanated, the father narrated the following story:

"We are water-bearers by profession and caste, and in four of our families in the village this boy is the only male child. Since his childhood his behaviour has been out of the ordinary. For years now he eats only once a month, sits for hours with his eyes fixed. Night after night he remains awake and yet neither his health nor his strength deteriorates. Some say he is possessed by some spirit; others say that he is mad; but none has any clue to his secret."

After a couple of months Ghauth Ali Shah revisited that village, and went to see the boy and his father. The boy was no longer there and the father, desolate and distressed, said, "It was the festival day after the fasting month of Ramadan. We asked the boy to put on new clothes and accompany us for prayers outside the village as was our custom. He came with us and, as we left the village behind, he separated from us and started to follow another path that led into the forest nearby. I left my other relatives and, concerned about my son's state of mind, followed him.

"He walked and walked and I walked with him until we reached a land of which I had never seen the like. As he walked, several animals and birds came near, stopped and greeted him, and then moved away, as though they all knew him and respected him. Then, after a couple of hours, he came upon a vast tree, and he stopped and sat down, speechless, with his eyes fixed as usual and calm as always. Birds and other animals of the land came and encircled him, greeted him and left. After some time an old man appeared from nowhere and brought me some food and water.

"After a few days, I could bear it no longer. So I addressed my son and pleaded with him to talk to me and tell me what I should do, and how long I should wait for him to return home. He then turned towards me, and wept. Holding my hand, he said, 'You go back, and leave my affair to God – I have been created for some other purpose.' So I left him and came away."

Ghauth Ali Shah soon came across another strange man in one of the princely states of north-west India. The raja was so devoted to this holy man that he had ordered a simple bamboo cottage to be built for his residence.

When the cottage was ready, he was escorted by those whom the raja had appointed to serve and look after him, and as he stepped into the cottage he asked, "Whose house is this?"

"It is your house."

As soon as he heard the sound of the words, "your house", he ran out in panic, lit a torch, came running back, committed the cottage to fire and watched it be consumed by flames and turned to ashes. When Ghauth Ali Shah came upon the scene, the third cottage was being built, and those who were in charge of this absurd task were sure that this too was going to be destroyed by the madman.

Ghauth Ali Shah watched how skilfully the cottage was being rebuilt with the prospect clear in the hearts of its builders that it would soon be destroyed at the hands of the very person for whom they were building it. So Ghauth Ali Shah said to them, "When you escort this unruly man into the cottage, do not answer his question about the ownership of the cottage by saying that it is his house, but instead say to him that it belongs to the king."

The suggestion worked and the cottage was saved. But although it was meant for his shelter and comfort, that strange man hardly used it. His behaviour was so unpredictable and enigmatic that nobody could feel settled in his company.

During one of the rare moments when he appeared sane and calm, Ghauth Ali Shah approached him and asked his name. He replied, "Nakku Kumhar" [lit. Foolish Potter]. When asked about his family, he mumbled something by which Ghauth Ali Shah deduced that he belonged to the Prophet's family. When asked about his age, he said, "One year and nine months."

Two years later, Ghauth Ali Shah learnt that the man died exactly twenty-one months after he had spoken to him. Thus he gave his remaining age, not the number of his past years.

So, during his travels, Ghauth Ali Shah witnessed many strange things, and met people whose speech and conduct were beyond custom or comprehension. At times he was critical; at other times he was just amused. But most of the time he bowed his head before each one of them, remembering that God was present to them all.

For the remaining eighteen years of his life Ghauth Ali Shah stayed in one place, at Panipat outside Delhi.

3

Encounters with Hindu Sages

As mentioned earlier, Ghauth Ali Shah learned Sanskrit from Pandit Ram Sanihi, who also acquainted him with the Vedas and Shastras, including the Gita and Upanishads [Hindu sacred texts]. His wet nurse, Pandit Ram Sanihi's wife, called him by a Hindu name, Ganga Bishan, and thus enabled him to have a sense of belonging with the names and symbols from the Hindu community and heritage. Hence, Ghauth Ali Shah showed respect and willingness to learn and to be influenced and transformed whenever he came before a Hindu sage or ascetic. Already we have referred to his initiations into several Muslim and Hindu mystical dimensions, and his teachers included both faqirs and sanyasis. Whenever he refers to Bengali faqirs, it is probable that he means Hindu sanyasis who were versed in alchemy and magic. Most of his allusions to the Hindu mystical life relate to the techniques and powers of concentration and control of breath.

During his adolescence, he says, he had his first encounter with a sanyasi who taught him how to control and suspend his breathing. The practice results in the ingathering of the soul, anulling all outgoing senses so that one can have utmost concentration on whatever one focuses one's attention upon. In his excitement at learning this powerful technique, Ghauth Ali Shah experimented on one of his younger brothers. The poor boy soon became unconscious and seemed to have passed away. The sanyasi was approached and brought to assist the boy to recover his consciousness.

When he sat up under the healing touch of the sanyasi, the boy first appeared to be in a trance and then, having fully recovered his senses, said that while we watched him lying unconscious he was from his viewpoint shouting to us that he was alive, that he was inside a deep well, that he should be lifted up.

Around the same time Ghauth Ali Shah underwent another mystical shock. One day his father took him to one of the elders of the Chishtiya Sufi order. During their session of devotional music, the elder looked at Ghauth Ali Shah with such concentration that he was neither conscious nor unconscious, and he felt as if all his knowledge had been wiped out. For nearly nine days, Ghauth Ali Shah says, I could not gather my senses. The benefit of that experience was such that whenever someone tried to look at him with similar concentration he remained impassive and, even when he was shaken for an instant or two, his knowledge was not touched.[1]

Among several incidents involving the Vedantic dimensions of spiritual practice and power, Ghauth Ali Shah recalls how as a young boy he once accompanied a cobbler's son on one of his mysterious visits in the night to the River Ganges where he used to practise Siddhi yoga and manifested strange powers.

During his wanderings in his early youth he met a Muslim who told him an extraordinary story. This man had left his village almost penniless in search of livelihood. After travelling for the whole day, he entered the outskirts of a town. As it was getting dark, he decided to stay there the night and recommence his search for work in the morning. He was approached by a prostitute. When

---

[1] The techniques of concentration practised by the Vedantic sanyasis and the Muslim faqirs are noticeably similar. They shared the doctrine of the ingathering of attention with or without control of breath which aimed at four distinct results: (1) concentration annulling both consciousness and knowledge, (2) concentration wiping out consciousness without affecting knowledge, (3) concentration suspending outer senses but heightening consciousness and deepening knowledge, and (4) concentration, present within, always at hand along with normal senses and consciousness – the last being the highest attainment.

he told her that he had no money even to eat, she went away but soon returned and said she could lend him ten rupees so that he could eat and have some money left for his journey. She said she did not mind when he paid her back, perhaps on his return when he again passed through that place.

With that money he travelled, got several jobs, did some trading and within a few years had earned a fortune. So he decided to return home. As he passed through the village where he had received such compassion from the prostitute, he thought of visiting her to repay his debt. But when he enquired after her, he was told that she had been unwell for some time and had passed away. He resolved to visit her grave as an act of remembrance of her kindness and of his gratitude.

Standing beside her grave with his heart full of tears and his eyes closed, he saw a door. He was asked to enter. Inside was a vast and beautiful garden with a mansion at its centre. He saw his benefactor fresh as the morning breeze walking towards him. She smiled and said, "All this is the reward for that little act of mine that night when my heart was moved by your poverty and I helped you with whatever I could." Then she talked to him about the beauties and the vastness of the world she had entered after her death. All of a sudden she looked concerned and asked him to close his eyes and return to his world. "For every moment spent here," she said, "a vast time will pass in your world."

When he opened his eyes, he was standing in a busy street with all sorts of strange people. There was neither grave nor graveyard. Everything had changed. He saw an old man looking at him with interest. As he approached him to ask where he was and what had happened while he had stood, his eyes closed only for a couple of minutes, the old man said, "One hour there is a hundred years here!"[2]

---

[2] It appears that up to the mid-nineteenth century there existed a vast mystical-magical culture that was shared by both the Hindus and the Muslims. As in Indian music, so in magic and meditation they learnt from one another. Ghauth Ali Shah speaks of his cousin having learnt how to have power over the snakes, which he learnt from a Bengali magician.

As we have mentioned earlier, Ghauth Ali Shah was nursed during his infancy by a Hindu lady. She had a son whom Ghauth Ali Shah regarded very highly. Once he accompanied his Hindu brother on his pilgrimage to Hardawar to have the sacred bath in the Ganges. Ghauth Ali Shah said that during this pilgrimage he learned the *Brahma Gayatri* [see Glossary for full text] which he recited in its ritualistic mode along with other pilgrims. There they came across two *pram hans*, sanyasis who were so absorbed and ingathered that they remained impervious to any hurt inflicted on their bodies. They were lying semi-naked by the river. In order to test them, somebody placed burning coals on their bare thighs. They neither moved nor showed signs of pain by any other gesture. Ghauth Ali Shah noticed that only one of them suffered from severe burns, whereas the other had no sign of any burns at all. When he raised the question with those who were watching this strange sight as to who was superior in his powers, most of them pointed to the man who had suffered no severe burns as the one who had greater power. But Ghauth Ali Shah disagreed and said that, in reality, the one who suffered the burns was greater as he was so self-absorbed that he was not aware what hurt was inflicted upon his body, whereas the one who had no burns at all cared about his body and exerted his inner powers to protect it from harm. Such a high degree of self-attainment is found, Ghauth Ali Shah says, in one person in a million, and is comparable with some of the spiritual elders in the Muslim tradition. There is another aspect of greatness with such people: they are not uplifted by those who are devoted to them, nor are they displeased with those who place burning coals upon their seemingly weak and starving bodies.

Ghauth Ali Shah gave another interesting account of his participation in the Hindu rites in Hardawar. A brahmin from his town, also visiting Hardawar, recognized Ghauth Ali Shah and advised him to be careful as the sacred rites were not permitted to non-brahmins. But he raised another question, why Ghauth Ali Shah had taken all that trouble to go to Hardawar and behave like a brahmin pilgrim while God was present in Islam and everywhere. Is it not really amusing, he asked, that each religious tradition regards the other as false and considers itself as the only truth? But if we rise above the diversity and the opposition of religious symbols we may look at them as pointing to the mystery of the same Reality which is one and simple. Ghauth Ali Shah then explained to him that he had taken the sacred bath in the Ganges on behalf of and for the benefit of Pandit Ram Sanihi whose wife had fed him during his infancy.

Ghauth Ali Shah referred to another brahmin pandit from Hardawar, Sarun Nath, who taught him how to recite Gayatri and meditate upon it. Gayatri begins and ends with the sacred monosyllable *Om*, as though pointing to the fact that the beginning and end (and also the middle for those who know) are undifferentiated unity and simplicity.[3]

Ghauth Ali Shah regards the Sanskrit monosyllable Om as representing the same Reality as the Qur'anic word for the Godhead, *Allah*. Gul Hasan gives the following rendering of the Gayatri:

Om! Allah! One who gives to those who know Him everlasting happiness;
One whose Being is reflected in all His creation and who keeps them under limit and measure;
One who is the Bestower of all existence and honour;
He alone is worthy of affirmation and worship.
His light is pure form, reflected in souls, and in which they find their rest.
Truly, we believe that our five senses, our reason and our heart are all turned to their Source.
We pray that we are made pure, that we incline to Him alone!

[3] The actual Sanskrit text of the Gayatri as given in the Glossary does not begin with the invocation of Om. Gul Hasan uses this invocation as an introductory or initiatory sound to utter the supreme Word, *Allah*, which represents All-Being and Beyond-Being. He thus bears witness to the eclectic spirit of his Master by reciting in one breath "Om" and in another breath "Allah", both as inhalings of the innermost secrets of self. He takes similar liberty in translating the Gayatri and almost islamicizes it.

During the last quarter of the night after Ghauth Ali Shah had done the meditation on the Gayatri he saw in his dream a vast and splendid assembly right in the middle of the Ganges: a celestial congregation of prophets and saints in two groups of equal glory facing each other. One group was headed by the Prophet of Islam, and the other group was led by [the Hindu god] Shri Krishna.

The latter said to the Prophet, pointing to Ghauth Ali Shah, "Kindly make him understand!"

Thereupon the Prophet said, "It is better if you tell him."

Then Krishnaji turned towards Ghauth Ali Shah and said: "What is lacking in your house that you search somewhere else? Do you still think that there are two houses? Everywhere Reality is one. We differ only in the words we speak."

When Ghauth Ali Shah asked Pandit Sarun Nath, who had taught him the Gayatri, about his mystical journey, Sarun Nath narrated the following story.

At an early age, said Sarun Nath, "I was gripped by the desire to leave my home and family and enter into the service of a guru." So one day he left his home and village and, after long wanderings for several days, he reached Hyderabad [in south India] where he learnt about a holy man who had a vast number of disciples. He was an old man. At the time Sarun Nath reached him, he was very ill and was dying. All his disciples, tired of his illness and old age, had left him. He was alone and helpless. Sarun Nath felt so drawn to him that he decided to stay with the old man and serve and nurse him.

When the old man's final moment in this world was near, he asked Sarun Nath to draw closer, and then instructed him in the six words of power whose meanings were not known but whose powers were extraordinary. They are like the mysterious letters which appear at the beginning of certain chapters in the Qur'an.

Sarun Nath told Ghauth Ali Shah that, after the old man had passed away, he came to Hardawar, meditated upon those mysterious words several nights by the River Ganges, and found in them great powers and freedom from want and fear. "Though I could not achieve [the path of] poverty," said Sarun Nath, "I was given the riches of both worlds without pride or hardness of heart."

Once Ghauth Ali Shah was passing through Dehra Dun where, on one of the mountains, he met a Muslim faqir who, over the years, had been practising Vedantic [Hindu] forms of meditation. When asked what difference he found between the Islamic and the Vedantic modes, he replied that there was none except that of terminology. Ghauth Ali Shah however noticed a greater emphasis among the Hindu faqirs on alchemy and use of herbs, through spiritual insight, for healing. Amidst all the variety and at times highly enigmatic practices of his Hindu brethren, Ghauth Ali Shah could reach the essence of Vedantic purity. It was this openness of heart that once made a brahmin give him, in confidence, the following mantra:

> Link your attention with God so that all the desires of your
>   heart and senses are burnt in its fire.
> Let the worshipper worship God with humility, contentment
>   and steadfastness so that all hopes and fears are set aside.
> When all attention is absorbed in God, one's being is like a
>   fragrant flower.
> Whoever has said this has indeed spoken the truth.

From his encounters with Hindu rishis and sadhus, Ghauth Ali Shah could see a clear distinction between those who had reached a level of self-attainment through contemplative practices and meditation on Gayatri and those who, though possessing strong concentration, had developed powers to influence other people's reason, will and imagination. Once Ghauth Ali Shah came across a Hindu boy who, in spite of his young age, had extraordinary powers of concentration to influence people and override their reason and will to make them act as he willed. But when he came face to face with a man of God, he paused, and said to Ghauth Ali Shah, "No, not this man; he is among those who are awake!"

After a couple of days Ghauth Ali Shah met another Hindu, a

gardener outwardly but a man of great attention inwardly. He taught Ghauth Ali Shah a mantra by which he could realize whatever he would wish and will.

Once while passing through Jodhpur, Ghauth Ali Shah heard of a Hindu faqir who had until recently stood day and night for twelve years. Ghauth Ali Shah searched for him, and when he found his house and knocked at his door, a young man with a pale face opened the door.

On inquiry the young man said, "Yes, Stranger! I am that same man who stood day and night for twelve years, and a world used to come and watch me, including the raja, all sitting at my feet with great devotion; but now nobody comes or even looks at me because now I am married and I behave like them and I walk as they do."

Having seen the vast variety of spiritual phenomena and people's attitudes to miracles and holy men, Ghauth Ali Shah was now on his way to Mecca for his pilgrimage when he came across a Hindu faqir who was accompanied by four of his disciples. "As I came to know him," Ghauth Ali Shah said, "I developed a sense of belonging to him, as if we were old friends." When Ghauth Ali Shah asked him about concentrating the mind during meditation, the faqir said that he would talk about such matters on the fourth day of their fellowship. He made Ghauth Ali Shah fast for three days, and in the early morning of the fourth day, as promised, he transmitted to Ghauth Ali Shah a light from within himself. Its effect was instantaneous; Ghauth Ali Shah felt his heart fill with an unearthly happiness and a strength that he would never lose.

It was near Bhopal [in central India] that Ghauth Ali Shah met a Hindu faqir, Satil Das, who asked him to fast for three days, after which he would impart the secret of ingathered attention. Keeping his promise, on the fourth day, he asked Ghauth Ali Shah to sit before him. As he looked at him, Ghauth Ali Shah saw a mighty flame leap from the space between himself and Satil Das and reach high above them. In its light, he saw his body as a transparent globe of glass and the whole world in it, everything far having come near. Ghauth Ali Shah was impressed but, at the end of that powerful session, he said to Satil Das, "Real vision is the seeing of one's own self, not of something that is other than self."

4

Encounter with Gul Hasan

Gul Hasan gives the following account of his life's journey leading to his encounter with Ghauth Ali Shah Qalander and his subsequent relationship with him as his friend and guide and a co-traveller on the path of truth and union with truth.

I had no real desire to study any books, even after I had passed the thirteenth year of my life. It was all fun and games. There was no worry nor any need to exert one's mind. My father, though aware of my inaptitude for any kind of studies, was kind to me, and did not press me beyond a point until the time came when he thought that I would willingly go to Rawalpindi where I could attend the school under the tutelage of one of his friends. After a year or so, I took my examination, which I passed, and then joined service in one of the departments of the government, and yet my original nature which never took anything seriously allowed me to remain unburdened by any concerns for my future.

Then one day some of my friends asked me to accompany them on a visit to a certain Sufi master; they intended to enter his circle and give their oath of allegiance to him. I had no idea who that Sufi Shaikh was and what they really meant about joining his circle. I was mystified at the mention of the oath of allegiance to be given to a stranger. Yet I agreed to accompany them without knowing what effect it could have upon me. Without hesitation I followed them and gave my oath of allegiance to that man and returned. I was soon immersed in my routine work, having set aside the entire episode of joining a mystical circle.

Seven years passed and, as I entered my twenty-first year, a strange unrest gripped my heart. It seemed that I was wasting my life in that employment, and one day I left the job and just went out into the world without knowing where I was going. After a night's journey I entered the district of Multan. The shrine of Sultan Bahu [c. 1691] is situated a few miles north-west of the city of Multan. As I approached the shrine, I decided to stay there until I received some guidance, some hint about my journey. Sultan Bahu's shrine was famous for providing guidance, particularly for those who had no idea where to go.

Twelve days passed, each day like the last. There was no sign and neither was there peace within me. My sense of distress was so great that I was about to lose hope. I used to see a madman hovering around the shrine, perhaps a majzub, one who is absorbed all in God and has no reason left to relate to the world.

One day as I was sitting in great distress, he came near me and said, "Gul Hasan, listen!" I was taken aback, thinking: how could he know my name? He said to me, "Do not lose heart. The emperor has gone to Delhi; soon after his return, we will present you to him. Now take rest."

I understood by "emperor" he meant the soul of Sultan Bahu whose shrine it was. Without giving me any more time to think, he asked me to follow him into the adjacent garden, where he plucked one of the roses and placed it upon my head. I had no idea why he did that. After some time, he said to me that it was time for prayer and we should go and pray. While I offered my prayers, I was aware that he was sitting nearby and talking nonsense, either to himself or to some invisible companion.

Then he left me until the next day when he appeared from

nowhere and said to me, "Come, the emperor has returned!" He took me by the hand into the shrine and made me stand before the tomb. We both were standing as if before the throne of a living emperor. Then he said to the tomb as if addressing the soul of the saint, "This man, Your Majesty, is very anxious for his head to be cut off." Then he started talking some other kind of nonsense which was beyond my comprehension. All of a sudden, he stopped and turned to me and said, "Well, the emperor has given you permission to leave, you can go." There was no clue where to go, or with what end. The entire episode, however nonsensical, had a certain awe-inspiring aspect. So I came away never seeing that madman again, but that night when I slept I had a dream. I saw Sultan Bahu, or someone who I thought was Sultan Bahu, asking me to go towards Delhi. When I woke up it was my fifteenth day at the shrine. Soon I reached Delhi.

On the fifth day after I arrived in Delhi, I had a feeling that I should leave Delhi and go to Lahore. As I was going through Panipat, a city a few miles to the west of Delhi, I sensed a strange freshness in its air, my depression was soon lifted and I thought of staying at Panipat for a few days. At night I stayed at the shrine of Bu Ali Shah Qalander [d. 1323] and in the day would wander in the streets of the city. After a couple of days I had a dream. I saw an elderly man, his face alight, his beard white, who asked me to visit the shrine. When I awoke, I assumed it was my own imagination returning to me in the form of a dream. After the third day he appeared again in my dream and insisted that I go on visiting the shrine. When I awoke I set aside the dream once more and tried not to pay any attention to it. After three more days the same figure appeared in the dream, furious at my indifference to his request.

I said to him, "I am staying in Panipat to study and learn; I cannot waste my time hanging around the shrine." The old man was even angrier than before and said that if I didn't obey him, he would break my neck. When I awoke, my heart was pounding with a strange fear or apprehension. I could not understand who he was and why he was after me, why he wanted me to spend more time around the shrine.

So it was on that day some time in the afternoon that I visited the shrine, went inside and offered my prayers at the tomb, came out and sat down on the seat made of red stone near the fountain and continued watching the water rising to a few feet and falling back.

After some time, I don't remember how long after, I noticed a man of noble bearing, a strange blend of human and celestial dignity, approaching me. How could I know that this was the man with whom I was going to stay for several years to come, who was going to be my mentor and master? As he came near me, he looked at me and said, "Salaam 'alaikum". I returned the greeting. Then he asked where I had come from and why I had come to Panipat.

However impressed I was by the stranger's appearance, I was in no mood to indulge in polite conversation for the sake of it. I was already agitated, so I replied, "Why are you asking me these questions? What is it all to do with you?"

Then he said, "Your face seems to be that of a traveller and I am also a traveller. Like you, I am also a newcomer here; one traveller looking upon another traveller feels happy that he has company. My heart says that I should hear your story and tell you my story so that we could come to know each other."

I was still upset; I could not understand why he was after me, so, in a state of uncertainty, I said, "Stranger, I am not the only traveller in this town; there are so many out there. You may call any one of them and talk to them."

Seeing my continued unfriendliness, he laughed and said, "Now I cannot leave you; now we are set for each other! Let us go somewhere and settle down and have a proper fight."

For some reason, I agreed and followed him. And as I walked with him, I repented in my heart that, while he talked to me with love and kindness, I treated him with indifference and unfriendly words. I placed before him all that I had gone through and why he found me there, sitting outside the shrine.

Thereupon he said, "Whatever work you have, you may continue, but come and see me at least once a day. I am not asking much." Then he taught me how to invoke God's blessings upon the Prophet and his Family and said that this invocation would remove the heaviness from my heart. I left him then having first asked his forgiveness for the way I treated him in the beginning.

As I continued to meet him every day, my love and regard for him took possession of my soul and, each time I met him, my life became more meaningful as I saw the significance of my love for him. It was the yearning in the heart of the disciple to receive enlightenment, and confirmation of his enlightened state, at the hands of his master. He always asked me never to lose patience and for every new knowledge received one should give something in charity. Whenever I asked him for some meditation to practise he laughed and suggested that I become accustomed to spending time in ruins, in places no longer inhabited by humanity.

One day I insisted on receiving some meditative practice from him. Thereupon he said, "You may start today after midnight at the doorway of the shrine of Bu Ali Shah Qalander. It is better if you start a little after midnight; by that time I will be alone and will hold you in my attention."

Then he gave me the following zikr whose awe and majesty was such that I trembled as I heard it in his voice.

Sufficient is my Lord as all power belongs to God.
There is no one in my heart other than God.
The light of Mohammed is all blessed by God.
There is no god but God.

I started this zikr at the suggested place and, after the midnight hour was passed, a strange unconsciousness came upon me; although my eyes were closed I saw a black snake of awesome size, with eyes fiery and bright, circle around me three times, then come near and rest its head upon my thigh. I was so frightened that my rosary fell from my hand and the snake lifted its head and opened its hood and stood before me, its eyes fixed upon my face.

After a time I gathered my courage and said to him, "Whoever you are, I should tell you that I am not sitting here of my own accord; I have been asked to sit here. It is up to you whether to harm me or to go your way." As soon as I uttered these words the snake withdrew and slowly slipped into one of the spaces near the threshold at the doorway of the shrine.

Somebody whom I knew was sleeping a little away from me; he got up, perhaps awakened by my disturbance. When I told him about the snake, he picked up his staff and started to look around but there was no trace whatsoever of any snake.

Soon after this, I resettled and continued the zikr till the time of morning prayers. Thinking that I should now prepare for the prayer, I kept the rosary on the floor and started to set my turban and then, as I picked up the rosary, it was not the rosary but a snake that I held. I cried out in alarm and threw down the snake but what fell was the rosary, the beads of which were now scattered. Totally shocked and exasperated, I entered the mosque, offered my prayers and then called upon my master.

As soon as he saw me approaching him he smiled and said, "What was all that hustle and bustle last night?'"

When I told him of my encounter with the apparition of the snake, he remarked, "Indeed, when you play a tune upon a flute, you will attract its corresponding form. All snake-charmers know this."

To which I replied, "If this is how the snake is linked with the flute, I shall have to give up the ghost one day or the other."

He started laughing. When I asked what it was that assumed the form of the snake he smiled and said, "All these are the disguises of the qalander." I was not sure to which qalander he was referring, whether to Bu Ali Shah Qalander or to himself.

Then one day he gave me a book and asked me to go through it and make use of it. Within it, I found prayers and meditations which, with concentrated practice, would enable one to meet Khizr in one's dream. Later Ghauth Ali Shah also taught me how to concentrate on the praise of the Prophet in one's heart so that one may see the Prophet in one's dreams. I was blessed three times by the Prophet's vision and was assured of attaining my heart's desire. As I reported these experiences to him he said that I would soon see the Prophet in reality on my way to Medina though I would not be able to recognize him. Once I asked him about concentration and its reward. He replied, "As far as the written word is concerned, it is said that when the initiator strikes the heart of the initiate with the zikr of Allah, then a light issues forth from the heart of the master and enters the heart of the disciple which becomes the seat of his concentration and the stabilizer of his state. Another kind of concentration by the initiator is described as unitary; the master identifies himself with the initiate. They become a unity, an identity of attention and state; all difference or otherness falls away. Such attention lasts for ever; its state is beyond any dispersal."

Several days later, as I slept at night, a vision or a dream unfolded before me. It was a tomb of some spiritual elder or sage. On the west of the tombstone, I saw Ghauth Ali Shah seated in the posture to perform zikr and on the eastern side I saw a majzub of moderate height, brown complexion, broad forehead, curly hair and beard turning grey. They were facing each other and were occupied with some contemplative meditation. As I found myself in their company, I said: "Salaam 'alaikum." Ghauth Ali Shah pointed towards the other person as if I should go towards him. After some hesitation he asked me to sit down, and soon, looking at my heart, he exclaimed, "Hu!" ["That", the Transcendent Absolute] with such force that I felt as if lightning had struck me. When I regathered myself after that shattering experience, I heard myself to my own amazement saying that I was not satisfied. Thereupon the majzub pointed towards Ghauth Ali Shah. I turned towards him and he looked at me with such a piercing glance that I became almost unconscious. Regathering my senses, I insisted that I was not satisfied. Then I was told that if I asked more I had to lose my life. I said that this was precisely my heart's desire. He then looked at me with such power that all my self-awareness was wiped out. When I was mysteriously brought back to my senses I insisted in my madness that I required more than what I had been given. I was told that if I did receive more my heart would not bear it.

Then I woke up. I was drenched in cold sweat from every fibre of my being. I could hear the zikr of Allah inside me and the condition of my heart was as if it was going to leap out of my body. When I looked at my body it was like a transparent glass and, wherever I looked from east to west, nothing obstructed my view, all heaven and earth were before me. I could not decide whether such a witnessing was a part of my dream or was all a state of wakefulness.

I stayed in this state for perhaps an hour or two, then returned to my normal state. I rushed to the mosque for the morning prayers and there I saw him standing in the doorway of the mosque, smiling at me. I could not control myself and started asking him one question after another. I asked him, "Had you not once said that one glance by a sage is enough to create a state for everlasting time? And if this is so, why was it that my state lasted for only a couple of hours, although each of the pair I encountered was a perfect sage?"

He listened to me in great calm, remained silent for some time and then said, "It was the effect of the soul upon the soul; it is a great thing that your body manifested that effect even for two hours. It is not possible for any ordinary humans to have the effect for such a long time while they are in body. Had this attention been with that force from one body to another, your body would have long been burnt to ashes."

To which I submitted, "What about this moment, sir, when there is a body on both sides?"

Ghauth Ali Shah smiled and kept quiet.

Now my life was knit with the fabric of knowledge which I

received in my service and devotion to Ghauth Ali Shah. Whatever time I had away from him, I spent in study, acquainting myself with the books of Qur'anic exegesis, Prophet's traditions (hadith), Islamic law, logic and philosophy. But whenever I approached him I left behind all those books and placed myself in his presence as a clean slate. It was up to him to make any imprint upon my mind. That is how I understood the meaning of discipleship, but he always postponed it by sending me to one or other learned man in the vicinity.

When I first asked his permission to go on pilgrimage to Mecca and Medina he asked me to postpone it for a while. Then, at last, he gave me permission.

After completing my *Hajj* [pilgrimage to Mecca], I decided to go to Medina to lay my head at the Prophet's shrine. I thought it would be a sign of disrespect if I travelled by any other means except on foot. So I started out and, after covering a few miles on foot, my feet were so swollen and the pain was such that I could not walk even a few steps. Then I knew that I had reached the end of my life and it was perhaps destined that in this vast desert, without water or grain, all alone I would breathe my last, thus deprived of the Prophet's shrine.

As my eyes were filling with tears, I noticed from one side of the desert a strange cloud of dust moving towards me. Out of that cloud emerged a company of horsemen headed by a Turk. They stopped, enquired after me, then attended to my wounds. The Turk, who seemed to be the leader of the company, asked one of his men to take me to a caravan that was going towards Medina so that someone could take me on his camel to my destination. During my journey I looked for that Turk and even asked for him and about his identity. But neither did I see him again nor would anyone tell me who he was. When I reached Medina I remembered what Ghauth Ali Shah had told me: that one day I would encounter the Prophet in person but would not recognize him.

After my second pilgrimage, Ghauth Ali Shah agreed to accept my discipleship and to bind me within the mystical order of Naqsh-bandis. During this period, I noticed how he treated whoever came unto him with such generosity and compassion so that everyone after leaving him was filled with faith and hope. He influenced people from a distance, healed and instructed sometimes directly and sometimes through one of us who were close to him. He knew the art of joining the hearts of his friends and disciples in spite of their diverse temperaments and styles of life.

Then a time came when I continued to stay in Panipat and vis-ited him every day. He expected me every evening to eat with him. The kindness he had shown me in the first meeting continued undi-minished and uninterrupted for the rest of our fellowship. Almost every month once or twice I would become upset or annoyed at something or other. Then he would send one of his attendants to fetch me. When I arrived in his presence, he would embrace me and say, "You are a traveller and I am also a traveller. Travellers should not fight; they should continue their journey, reconciling and rec-onciled." There was so much peace in those tasteful resentments and ecstatic reconciliations. Now he is gone, leaving behind mem-ories and tears. With whom should one fight now and with whom be reconciled?

5

Intimations of the End

Seven months before he left this world, as Gul Hasan tells us, Ghauth Ali Shah started having intimations of his forthcoming end.

We had all seen the new moon of the fasting month of Ramadan. We all attended the prayers that evening as Ghauth Ali Shah himself led them. After the prayers were over, while he was sitting by himself with nobody around him, he called me and asked me to sit near him. Then he said, "Listen to me, I am going to tell you certain things which are very important. When I first came to Panipat, I withdrew at the shrine of Bu Ali Shah Qalander and sat in meditation for forty nights as advised by Sayyid Azam Ali Shah, one of the spiritual elders for whom I had a very high regard.

"It was the last night of my meditation at some late and still hour that I saw, as if in a vision, a man, apparently mad, of brown complexion and curly hair, standing before me, and he said that he would like to instruct me. Then another man appeared who was fair with a white beard, wearing a long green garment and holding a staff. He said that neither he nor the other could teach me anything. 'Your affair', he continued, 'is beyond our teaching. Your affair is with the Divine Essence. Whatever shall happen to you will follow from how you relate to that Essence. Wipe out', he said, 'from your heart all the traces of the living and the dead. Nobody can give you anything. As you have turned towards that Ineffable Unseen, then go in that direction. Besides Beyond-Being you have neither any friend nor helper.

"'In your origin', he continued, 'you are a lover of that Essence of singularity and simplicity. In that love there is no room for association with any saint or prophet. Your affair is between you and God. You know it and He knows it. It is beyond our power to tell you more, except whatever is going to happen will happen within three, four, five and six, and then there is union!'

"In the morning I narrated this strange vision and communication to my elderly friend. Thereupon he wept, and said 'Ghauth Ali Shah! Almighty God is beyond all need and desire, and you will see what is before you.'

"'Why are you so distressed?' I asked. 'This is my affair with God, and I take rest in it. Should I not be happy that He has allowed me to reach Him alone, and liberated me from remaining in need of anyone else? Praise be to Him that He has made me His own. What more can one aspire for and hope to attain?'

"Then [said Ghauth Ali Shah] we added up those numbers. Their total was eighteen. First we thought they referred to eighteen days. When we entered the nineteenth day, we thought they referred to eighteen months. When we entered the nineteenth month, it became clear to us that the total of the numbers given in the vision should refer to eighteen years. My friend, Gul Hasan, I have stayed in Panipat for eighteen years since that vision. It means that this is the last year of my life here."

After that day when he told me that his end was near, he recited the following Qur'anic verse in every session almost each day: *The parable of those who take friends other than God is that of the spider, who builds to itself a house; but truly the weakest of houses is the spider's house if they but knew* [Q. 29.41].

After two months Ghauth Ali Shah called again and narrated to me a dream he had had a couple of nights before, and asked me to give its interpretation. He had seen three of his friends who had already left this world. They were all pious and God-fearing men. There they were in his dream, saying to him, "Your house is ready and we have the keys. You may come and see it."

Thereupon Ghauth Ali Shah replied, "Friends, we have not made any house anywhere. Wherever we lived, we lived homeless and, whenever we left, we left no traces behind. Like snakes we passed through houses built by others. So to what sort of house are you referring?"

But they insisted. So he accompanied them. They brought him before a beautiful mansion and opened the door for him. As he entered he found himself under a dome, and there he saw a locked casket. One of his friends said, "We do not have the key, for only your touch can open the casket."

As he opened it he found inside a multi-coloured ball made of silken wrappings. He started unwrapping the strange object and, finally, at the end of the last wrapping, found a beautiful little case. When he opened it, it was filled with musk with a fragrance that was so enchanting that he said to his friends he would like to stay. But they said, "Wait for a few more days – still a few more people have to benefit from you. Do not make haste."

After narrating the dream, Ghauth Ali Shah was silent for some time, and then looked at me and said, "Gul Hasan, you are good at interpreting dreams – tell me what it all means."

"I may not add much to what you already know", I said to him, "and therefore what I say to you is very little. The mansion you saw in your dream is the world. The dome represents your grave, and the casket, your body. The little beautiful case inside the coloured silken wrapping is your heart, and the musk can be nothing else but the nameless name of God."

On hearing all this, he first raised his hand as though saying that it was a dream. Then he took my hand in his hand in gratitude that perhaps I did interpret the dream rightly.

After a couple of weeks he called me again and said that he had another dream. I knew that it was going to be another intimation of his end. Noticing my sadness, he said, "What is it in a dream which touches us so much?" Then he smiled and said, "We are just testing your art because you know how to look through the veil of the images."

After a five-minute pause, he started narrating the dream: "I found a small casket in my lap and, when I opened it, I found inside a small insect of unknown identity. I took it out and gently placed it on the floor. It started moving, its colour becoming brighter, its wings sprouting from its body. Soon it spread its newly found wings and flew away."

He was silent. I knew it was the end of the dream. "It is very painful for me, dear master, to interpret this dream; the casket is your body and the insect is your soul. And, when the soul reaches its perfection, it can no longer stay imprisoned."

When I told him that my heart sinks while interpreting such dreams, he reminded me, "To be distressed is to disagree with the divine decree!"

After a month while he was sitting in the mosque amidst his friends and disciples, he turned to me and said, "The death of the body is inevitable. After my death you may cut my body into four pieces and scatter them so that at least some animals and birds can satisfy their hunger. What other use can one think of as far as a corpse is concerned? But, Gul Hasan, you will not be able to do that, nor would people allow you to do so. Therefore, bury us in some deserted place without the shade of any tree upon our grave where there is no support or shelter except that of God."

After a couple of days he fell sick. During that illness, one Thursday night, he asked us to leave him alone in his room and close the door. We all knew what it meant, and our hearts sank. We waited into the night, watching the closed door. It was about four in the morning when we heard his voice calling us to enter. A great burden was lifted from our minds. As we entered his room, he pointed to one of his friends to fetch for him some fresh pomegranate seeds, and then turned towards us and uttered four unrelated statements which nobody could understand:

"Whatever we had thought, it was not how it happened.

"Others also could reach only to this point.

"Neither the scholarship of the learned nor the labour of the washerman were of any benefit whatsoever.

"Friends, if we live five or ten years more, what difference will it make? But we will not live so long!"

For a few days he felt better. Then one day he called me and gave me ten rupees for his shroud and burial and reminded me that I should not take any money from anybody else and, if required to pay for the place of his burial, I should pay from my own resources.

One of the memorable instances of his last days was that a four-teen-year-old boy whose father was one of the disciples of Ghauth Ali Shah composed a lengthy poem in Persian in praise and love for him. We were all surprised at the literary excellence of the poem, and it brought to all of us great comfort at that time of great distress.

During all that illness, Ghauth Ali Shah remained stable, his face bright, his manner pleasant and his hospitality undiminished. Whoever came and asked about his health, he always said, "All praise be to God." It was at nine forty-five on Sunday night, the sixth of Rabi-ul 'Awwal, 1297 Hijra,[1] that he left this world.

[1] Corresponding to the Hindu calendar 12 Bhagun 1936 and Christian calendar 7 March 1880.

The Writer's Farewell to his Pen

O Pen! Rise again and walk with me a few more steps. You tell me your story and I will tell you my story.

That vast and nameless territory which was your native land and your habitat and all those changes of spring and summer, each following the other which once nourished you and tested your strength – where are they now?

The love for composing this book made you an exile, separated you from your kin, plucked you from the tree which was fresh and green. Then you allowed yourself to be imprisoned in a pen case waiting for a hand from the unseen to liberate you and bring you into the light of a new fellowship. The moment came when I picked you up, for whom you were created. Like you I am also an exile in a foreign land. I was also friendless and sad. We thus found in each other's company a connection and an extension of being.

But ah, my friend, the days of our fellowship were limited. The book which we both wrote together has now come to an end. Its last page has been written. Now this book bids you farewell. So long as you exist you will yearn for uniting with this book again, and like me you will also continue to weep in remembrance of our shared union with the words we so carefully wrote together.

O Pen! On this day our work and your labour are over. Let us say farewell to each other. Let us embrace each other for the last time. These few days of intimacy were a passing even under the constellations of the heavens. We do not know when and where we shall meet again, and where this book, the fruit of our love and devotion, will go. But the beauty of the script and the faithfulness of its flow, line after line, will remind every reader, O Pen, of your self-effacing commitment.

O Pen, you did not have the power of movement nor did I possess the strength to think these thoughts and put them into words. All these, along with their many meanings, are neither your invention nor my discovery. All these were the visions carved by the proficient artisan of life and wisdom. Neither have I the heart to praise their beauty nor have you the strength to describe them.

Today, on this day our work is completed whose beginning and end were both in the realm of the unseen.

O God, had you not guided me in love and friendship, these thoughts which were without form and limit in my soul could not have been expressed in the frame and measure of this book. O God, had you not held my heart in your hands it could not have received the seed of this tree. Had you not nourished this tree by the water of your grace, it could not have provided shelter to one who was burnt by the fire of separation.

14 Shaban 1301 Hijra [19 June 1884 AD]

Reference in Original Text

Glossary

Unless otherwise shown, the listed terms are Arabic.

Ahad. Qur'anic term for the Transcendental Unity/Oneness of the Godhead.

Ahadiyya. Transcendental Unity.

Ana. First person singular.

Arjuna (Sanskrit). The warrior figure of the *Bhagavad-Gita*, one who goes through crisis of judgment as to the meaning of war. Krishna is his chariot-driver representing his higher self. Arjuna is a symbol of human aspiration to self-knowledge and ultimate union with truth.

Arti puja (Sanskrit). Offering of lighted lamps before the symbolic image of a deity in the Hindu temple – lighted lamps being the symbol of life and consciousness of the devotee.

Avatar (Sanskrit). Divine incarnation.

Baqa. Sufi term for a state of everlasting being.

Batin. Qur'anic term for the hidden, the unmanifested; one of the Divine Names in the Qu'ran.

Baraka. Islamic term for blessing, grace, or sacred aspect or benefit.

Bhakti (Sanskrit-Hindi). Literally devotion, service. A mystical movement of the fourteenth to fifteenth centuries, universalist and humanist, with a blend of monistic and theistic emphases. It preached human equality and freedom from worldly status and social identity. Mathava (1302), Namdev (1344), Pipa (1425), Ramanand (1430), Ravidas (1430), Ramananda (1440), Mirabai (1504) and Kabir (1518) were some of the famous Bhakts who shaped the eclectic mood of medieval India in which the Sufi Masters, particularly the Chishtiyas, joyfully participated.

Brahma (Sanskrit). The Hindu god of creation.

Brahmin (Sanskrit). Member of the Hindu priest caste.

Caliph. Literally, successor; the caliphate dates from the Prophet Mohammed's death in 632 when successors were chosen to lead the community and extend the community and preserve Islamic law.

Chishtiya. One of the major Sufi orders, mainly Indian, having connections with Iran. Muinuddin Chisti (d. 1236) was the founder figure.

Faqir. Literally, one who is a beggar; in Sufi usage one who has attained the station of poverty (*faqiri*), who practises complete trust in God.

Fatiha. The short opening chapter of the Qur'an, beginning, *In the name of God, the Merciful, the Compassionate, Praise be to God, the Lord of the Worlds* ... It is an indispensable part of the daily worship (*salat*).

Gayatri (Sanskrit). Meditative chant/mantra used in the daily worship of

Hindus. Its transliterated text and translation is as follows.

Bhur bhuvah svah
tat savitur varenyam
bhargo devasya dhimahi
dhiyo yo nah pracodayat
santih santih santih

Body of all. Mind of all. Spirit of all.
May we meditate on the Supreme,
On the all-pervading radiance of the Primal Light.
May He inspire the innermost thoughts of our hearts.
Peace. Peace. Peace.

Ghauth. Literally, the Refuge; one of the Divine Names; also the popular title of Abdul Qadir Jilani (d. 1166), the founder-figure of the Qadriya Sufi order.

Hadith. Literally, story. Islamic tradition of sayings of the Prophet Mohammed and his companions, second in importance to the Qu'ran.

Hafiz. Literally, one who protects; one of the divine names; and also the popular title of one who has memorized a part or the whole of the Qur'an.

Hahut. The esoteric term for the realm of transcendence.

Hajj. Pilgrimage to Mecca made by every Muslim as a religious duty, at least once in their lifetime, if possible. One of the Pillars of Islam.

Haqiqat. The mystical-philosophical term for reality, as opposed to the unreal and contingent.

Hu. Third person singular; otherness/transcendence of God.

Ilah. The Qur'anic term for divinity; any object towards which one is totally inclined.

Il'l'Allah. Nothing but God; the affirmative end of the Islamic testimony "There is no god *but* God."

'Ilm. The Qur'anic term for knowledge as opposed to conjecture and opinion.

Imam. Literally, model; it refers to the leader of the worship (salat) and can be any upstanding male adult of the Muslim community; not a priest.

Iman. Faith, synonymous in meaning with knowledge; generally used in reference to faith in God, in life hereafter and in the unseen.

'Irfan. Gnosis; also means mysticism, esoteric philosophy in general.

Ithbat. Affirmation; primarily refers to the affirmative end of the Islamic testimony "There is no god *but* God", and also to the affirmation of the world as the meaningful and purposeful creation of God.

Jasrat. Father of the warrior-king (and avatar of Vishnu) Ram.

Jazb. Literally, absorption; in Sufi usage, a state of complete ingathering of the soul, an absorption, as it were, into the source of all-being. (*Jazba* is emotion by which one is absorbed by the object of the emotion involved.)

Ji. Honorific term suffixed to *pandit*, *guru* etc.

Jinn. The species created out of fire coupled in the Qur'an with humankind who are created out of clay. The Jinn are invisible to the human eye. They are capable of possessing humans. They are both good and bad, virtuous and vicious.

K'aba. The shrine at Mecca, said to have been built by Abraham (Ibrahim), which Mohammed cleared of idols and to which Muslims make their pilgrimage. It symbolizes the heart empty of anything other than God.

Kafir. The Qur'anic term referring to one who is ungrateful, one who rejects a prophetic call and actively opposes it.

Kashf. Literally, uncovering; in Sufi usage, attaining knowledge of the mysteries during contemplation.

Khizr. The Islamic representation of the figure of Elijah; in Sufi lore, one who guides without revealing one's true identity (but in the Qu'ran, Chapter 18, he identifies his spiritual station while Moses encounters him).

Krishna (Sanskrit). Literally, the Dark One. One of the most popular and playful Hindu gods; an incarnation of the god Vishnu. See also Ram.

Kufr. The state or act of ingratitude and rejection of God's bounty and grace.

Kun. The Qur'anic imperative "Be!" It stands for the divine command of creation.

Kwajha (Persian). Honorific title of Sufi shaikh.

La Ilaha. The negative part of the Islamic testimony "*There is no god*, but God."

Lahut. Sufi term for divinity: esoterically, divine otherness, a realm lower than hahut.

Laxman. Brother of the warrior-king (and avatar of Vishnu) Ram.

M'arifat. Gnosis, self-realization, recognition of truth.

Majzub. One who is in a state of jazb, spiritual absorption.

Mazkur. What is remembered, in reference to remembering God (zikr).

Mathnawi. The title of the six-volume corpus of mystical poetry by Jalaluddin Rumi (d. 1273).

Mithal. Literally, example; in Qur'anic usage, it refers to parables (plural *amthal*); and in the esoteric custom it represents the middle realm between the sensible and the intelligible worlds, *alam al-amthal*.

Mukashifa. The state of unveiling during contemplation; may also mean vision.

Nafi. Opposite of *ithbat*, affirmation; simple negation; as a term refers to the principle of *via negativa*.

Nafs. Quranic term for self, person, also soul in her individualized status. The Qur'an refers to humankind as *nafsin wahidah*, indivisible self, a psychic unity (4.1).

Naqshbandiya. One of the major Sufi orders, traces its identity to Baha'uddin Naqshband (d. 1390).

Om (Sanskrit). Also *Aum.* The Sanskrit monosyllable for the supreme invocation of undifferentiated reality.

Pandit (Sanskrit). Hindu scholar.

Pir (Persian). An old man; in popular custom, a sage/saint.

Qadri. One who belongs to the Qadriya order.

Qadriya. Order founded by Abdul Qadir Jilani (d. 1166).

Qalander (Persian). A wandering homeless sage; a Sufi master of high rank; in esoteric understanding, one who is directly initiated into gnosis by the Prophet, or Ali or Khizr (Elijah).

Qawwali. Devotional poetry and music sung primarily at the shrines of great masters; an Indian institution originating in the first half of the fourteenth century.

Qutb. Literally, the axis; in Sufi lore, the highest sage of the day, hidden from ordinary eyes.

Radha (Sanskrit). The cowherd girl who was the beloved of the Hindu god Krishna; she and the other cowherd girls who danced to his flute-playing represent the human soul in its dance before God.

Ram (Sanskrit). The warrior-king and hero of the *Ramayana.* One of the most popular incarnations of the Hindu god Vishnu.

Rishi (Sanskrit). Hermit/sage who has renounced the world; the secluded one, the individual.

Sadhu (Sanskrit). Literally, one who is without defect. Refers to a Hindu man who has renounced worldly life but remains independent of any order.

Salaam 'alaikum. Peace be upon you; the traditional Muslim greeting.

Salat. The sequence of utterances and actions of Muslim worship which is prescribed as one of the Pillars of Islam to be performed five times a day by all Muslims.

Samadhi (Sanskrit). Literally, ecstasy. It refers to the trancelike state induced through contemplation of and absorption into the unity of existence.

Sanyasi (Sanskrit). One who has renounced the world (feminine *sanyasin*).

Sayyid. Literally the leader, or head of a community. Traditionally, one who is a descendant of the Prophet from his daughter Fatima, from two of her sons, Hasan and Husayn.

Shaikh. Literally, elder; it refers to leaders and respected people in the community.

Shajrah. From Arabic *shajr*, meaning tree; in Sufi usage it refers to the tree of mystical connections, a symbol of spiritual genealogy.

Shariah/shariat. The Islamic law based on the Qu'ran and the prophetic tradition as interpreted by the jurists.

Shastras. Hindu books of legal codes and meditative techniques.

Shirk. Polytheism; the opposite of *Tawhid*, Divine Unity. Any association of the relative with the absolute.

Siddhi yoga. Meditation into a state of absorption in which psychic powers are developed.

Sufi. Derived from the Arabic root *safa*, meaning purity; one who has been purified, one who has a pure heart, or a heart which holds nothing but God's remembrance as presence.

Sufi order. A Western expression referring to a particular group of Muslim mystics with an identifiable set of rules and practices, not necessarily monastic.

Suhrawardiya. Sufi order founded by Abul Qahir Suhrawardi (d. 1168).

Tadhkira. Literally, a recollection; in literary usage, memoirs or collected works.

Tariqa/Tariqat. Qur'anic in origin, meaning way; in Sufic usage, an inner path with a master as the guide; in contrast to *shariah*, which is the outer path, *tariqat* means the principle of the inner path, a mystical doctrine.

Tawhid. The Islamic doctrine of the Oneness/Unity of God; the principle of monotheism.

Vedanta (Sanskrit). Literally, culmination of the Vedas, the ancient sacred texts of India. Technically it refers to one of the six orthodox philosophies of classical Hinduism, but is now used to refer more generically to classical Hinduism.

Zakir. One who is remembering God, through zikr. See below.

Zikr. Qur'anic in origin, meaning remembrance of God, along with fikr which is intellectual contemplation of the signs of God. In Sufi usage, it means a particular mode of remembrance, the recital of a divine name imparted to the novice for guidance and enlightenment.